# REDEMPTION

# REDEMPTION

## The Triumph of God's Great Plan

Derke P. Bergsma

Library of Congress Catalog Card Number: 89-37176

ISBN: 1-877607-12-6

Printed in the United States by:
Morris Publishing
3212 E. Hwy 30
Kearney, NE 68847
1-800-650-7888

"so that in everything HE might be supreme"

Colossians 1 : 18

To my faithful wife, Dorris.

# Contents

# *Preface*

THIS book grew out of a desire to present the message of the Bible in its marvelous coherence and unity. Sincere Christians and students of the Bible know much about the various parts of the Bible. They know the story of Creation, of the Flood, of the Exodus, of David and Goliath, Daniel in the lion's den, the birth of Jesus, many of His parables and miracles, and much more. But the essential theme of Scripture which knits all its parts together escapes many Bible readers. The relation between Old and New Testaments is especially obscure to many. I have been asked frequently, after leading church retreats and Bible conferences, to recommend something of manageable size to clarify the Bible's unifying theme. It is my hope that this book will help fill that need.

The guiding objective of this study is to understand each major part of the Bible in its relationship to the grand design of God's determination to save the world. It presents the "big picture," focusing especially upon Jesus Christ in whom the entire Scripture finds its unity. It moves from Genesis to Revelation, tracing the unfolding pattern which reveals God's love for a lost world and His determination to save it. It is organized along the lines of Biblical Epochs which are identifiable historical segments of the history of redemption. These Epochs are viewed, not as self-contained periods of Biblical history, but as parts of the story which build upon each other until they reach their climax in the life, death, and resurrection of Jesus Christ.

No work of this nature is ever a completely independent effort. It would be impossible to acknowledge all the sources to which I am indebted. Many of them have been lost in the process over the years in preparing class notes and lecture material. However, the shaping influence of Geerhardus Vos, especially his *Biblical Theology* should be noted. No theological writer has been more influential for my understanding of the Bible than he. For serious students the reading of a section of Vos is recommended at the end of most chapters. Vos' work is a much more complete review of the theology of the Scriptures than this book is designed to be. But both are intended to present the message of the Bible in its historical unity and organic wholeness. If this present work serves to stimulate interest in Biblical theology generally and the writings of Gerhardus Vos specifically, I shall be grateful. My fullest joy will be realized if knowledge of and interest in the Scriptures is increased as a result of this book.

Quotations from the Bible are from the New International Version with a few exceptions which are noted.

The graphic design which preceeds every chapter is intended to visually identify the particular segment of the history of redemption which the chapter covers. It should also help to grasp the sense of movement in the Bible's account of God's plan of salvation. The relationship between revelational epochs will be seen more clearly.

Scripture readings are recommended in connection with each chapter. The greatest benefit for the reader will be gained if the Bible passages are read first. Then the chapter should be read followed by a re-reading of the Bible selections. The Bible must always be the source of our Christian understanding and the final authority for the truth of God's solution for the human condition.

Study groups may find this book adaptable for their purposes. Individual Bible passages that are recommended for reading in connection with each chapter could be profitably studied as expansions of the book's material. Questions for the stimulation of discussion are included at the close of each chapter.

I wish to recognize with gratitude the gracious and competent help of Nora Gardner and Elaine Memmelaar in the preparation of the manuscript. Also, John Sale has provided invaluable help and advice for the graphic design that precedes each chapter. The encouragement of many who have attended retreats and conferences where I have lectured on Biblical history is also respectfully acknowledged. My wife, Doris, was among the most encouraging of them.

May the honor of the Lord and the blessing of many people be the result of this effort.

# JESUS CHRIST: The Focal Point of Scripture

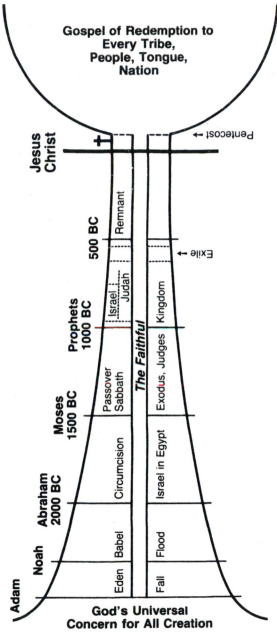

**Gospel of Redemption to Every Tribe, People, Tongue, Nation**

Jesus Christ

Pentecost →

← Exile

500 BC — Remnant

Prophets 1000 BC — Israel / Judah — Kingdom

The Faithful

Moses 1500 BC — Passover Sabbath — Exodus, Judges

Abraham 2000 BC — Circumcision — Israel in Egypt

Noah — Babel — Flood

Adam — Eden — Fall

**God's Universal Concern for All Creation**

# Introduction

### How Shall We Study The Bible?

The study of the Bible must be done with the recognition that Jesus Christ, His life, death, and resurrection, is the key to the understanding of the whole Scripture. In Christ, God's redeeming love is preeminently revealed, the testimony to which is the heart of Scriptural revelation. This is to say that the Bible alone tells us about a God who loved the world so much that He determined to save it through His Son Jesus. We can learn much about God's power and greatness by studying the natural world around us because He made it and His glory is reflected in it. But God's *grace*, His saving mercy toward a lost world is revealed to us only in the Holy Scriptures. In fact, the knowledge of God as revealed in the Christ of the Scriptures is an absolute necessity for the understanding of God as revealed in the natural order.

This book is an attempt to trace the message of the Bible from beginning to end with an unwavering focus on the centrality of Jesus Christ. It takes what has come to be known as a Biblical Theological stance. It may be called a thematic study of the Scriptures which attempts to discover the pattern emerging from the revelational record. It pays careful attention to the historical situations in which and through which God revealed himself with a view to understanding the total message especially as that message centers in Jesus Christ. Perhaps better said, it attempts to illuminate any particular passage of Scripture in the light of the total message. The guiding objective is to understand the role played by any one part of the Biblical message in the full account of God's grand design to redeem the world through His Son.

This study proceeds on the basis of some clearly assumed commitments regarding how we can know God and His will from the Bible. These commitments may be summarized in the following four statements:

1. God's revelation of Himself and His will is a *divine word and deed revelation*. God revealed Himself both through what He said and what He did. The Bible is an account of the self-revealing God speaking and acting to accomplish His redeeming purpose for mankind. It therefore demands a response of obedience from mankind to whom it is addressed. We must listen. We cannot modify it to fit our own ideas or society's interests.

2. The Bible is *historical* revelation. God's word and deed revelation addresses itself in the first instance to concrete, historical situations. The special, unique, historical context must be understood to properly interpret the various passages of the Bible.

3. The Bible is *redemptive* historical revelation. The Bible is an account of God's *saving* intentions for the world. This is its focus. It reveals what God determined to do and actually accomplished in redeeming a lost world to Himself. It is not a journal to be consulted for moral advice, although moral injunctions emerge in the process of revealing God's saving intention to call a people to live in fellowship with Himself.

4. The Bible is *progressive* redemptive historical revelation. It is not an all at once revelation, but moves from anticipation and promise (O.T.) to realization and fulfillment (N.T.) - from implicit to explicit, from bud to full-grown flower. But at whatever stage of its development, a single, consistent theme is evidenced throughout, namely, God's saving purpose for the world.

The use of the term Biblical Theology emphasizes our dependence upon the Bible for our theology. The word theology (Greek, *Theos Logos*) strictly interpreted means study or knowledge of God just as Biology is the study of life (Greek *Bios*) and Sociology is the study of human relationships (Latin, *Socius*). But God cannot be studied like plants and fellow human beings can, because God cannot be reduced to an object of human scrutiny. Theology, therefore, can be concerned with the knowledge of God only in so far as He has chosen to reveal Himself, since man, by searching (academic or otherwise) cannot discover the nature of God or even approximate such knowledge. The finite mind of man cannot comprehend God and if it were possible, human language is too inadequate a means to communicate such knowledge. No one knows the things of God except the Spirit of God, says the Apostle Paul (I Cor. 2:11).

And yet God, who is not amenable to human examination, has revealed Himself through his Word-Revelation which intrudes itself upon man and to which a response must be given. This faith response to the Word of God is either one of joyful obedience or antagonistic rebellion. There is no neutral ground. The theological task, therefore, is concerned with that which must be believed about God in his Word-Revelation and examines and systematizes man's response to it.

The term Word of God is far more comprehensive and inclusive than Bible. We recognize that the eternal Word of God by which all was created and is maintained in being could never be comprehended in a written record. Yet it is the Bible which is the only infallible guide which can illuminate clearly for us that universal Word which addresses man through all reality and should therefore give direction to all our study.

The mystery of the Bible as the product of human authors while at the same time constituting the Word of God is an irresolvable one. While remaining a mystery which belongs to the realm of faith and is therefore accessible only to faith, whenever the Bible has been accepted as Spirit-inspired and therefore God-given, believers have been a transformative force in the world. This was demonstrated during the Reformation as well as the period of the Great Century of Missions, 1795-1900. As Emil Brunner has observed, the fate of the Bible is the fate of Christianity. When the Bible is recognized as authoritative revelation, the Church exhibits vitality and a sense of purpose.

Throughout this study there is an implied affirmation of the essential unity of the Biblical record. It is not simply a collection of religious and moral writings produced by varieties of religiously sensitive Jews and Christians. It is a series of books recording a revelational account of the history of God's redemptive concern for the world, which culminates in Jesus Christ and anticipates an eventual Kingdom of righteousness and peace. Historical and linguistic distinctions between its parts are obvious, yet the essential message of the various parts follows a consistent theme. The purpose of this book is to clarify that consistent theme. The intention is not to give a detailed analysis of the Bible but to include detail only when necessary to illuminate the central theme.

# CHAPTER ONE

# *The Structure of Biblical Revelation*

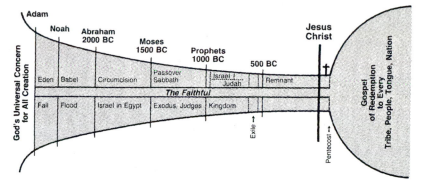

I. Major Events in Bible History.

    A. Creation of the Universe.

    B. Divine Response to Human Evil.

    C. Major Epochs.

        1. Adamic Epoch.
        2. Noahic Epoch.
        3. Abrahamic Epoch.
        4. Mosaic Epoch.
        5. Prophetic Epoch.
        6. Apostolic Epoch.

 II. Dating Revelational Epochs.

III. Divine Plan Met through Human Agents.

Scripture Readings
   Matthew 1
   Acts 7
   Hebrews 11

# The Structure
# of Biblical Revelation

THE Bible begins with the assertion, "In the beginning God created the heavens and the earth." This statement is the most all-inclusive, comprehensive, universal reference to reality one can possibly make. It includes everything that exists. It embraces the total universe. The Bible begins on a universal note. This is represented by the wide mouth of the funnel pattern in the diagram on the previous page.

As the message of the Bible continues, its concern is less and less with the total world and its people and more and more with a smaller and smaller group of human beings. The Bible focuses on those called to be faithful to the Lord as the ones through whom a Savior for the world could come. This group of obedient, faithful people became an increasingly smaller proportion of world population. When Jesus Christ arrived, as the hope of all the faithful preceeding Him, very few true believers remained. In truth one could say only Jesus was perfectly faithful. The narrowing of the funnel pattern serves to emphasize this fact.

The salvation accomplished by Jesus became the Good News which the Church has been commissioned to carry to the nations. No longer restricted to a narrowly defined group, it has universal application. Thus the Bible's message begins with the creation of the universe, narrows its focus till the promise of a Savior is realized, and then extends its focus to embrace salvation for the universe.

### Major Events in Bible History

Following the creation story (Genesis 1 and 2), the Bible proceeds to record the corruption of the universe as a result of the Fall of

9

Adam and Eve as the representatives of the human race who refused to live in obedience with their Maker. (Genesis 3) From that point on the Bible is an account of what God determined to do to save mankind and the world from its fallen state. God chose to reveal His plan of salvation to selected people who were called to be His agents through whom the salvation of the world would be realized. This selected group of agents had early on a very broad and inclusive character since all humanity is caught up in Adam. But among Adam's many children (Genesis 5:3 & 4) only Seth provided the continuity with the line of descendants who were agents of God's redemptive revelation. Many thousands of years later Noah and his family stood in the Sethite chain as the faithful line progressed. Of the three sons of Noah, only Shem was chosen as the one whose descendants were called to special responsibility for realizing God's saving purposes for the world. With Abraham one patriarchal family from among the Shemite heritage emerged as God's chosen servant, further restricting the human revelational agency.

The channel of redemption, or those chosen by God as agents to execute His plan of salvation, proceeded to narrow further after the time of Abraham. (c.2000 B.C.) With Isaac and then Jacob the realization of the promise of salvation for the world was restricted to the agency of a single nation (Genesis 26-50). At this point the nation of Israel, descendants of Jacob, were the chosen people, called to be faithful to the Lord, so that from among them would ultimately come the world's Savior. The identity of the nation of Israel as God's agents of redemption continued in Biblical history through four hundred thirty years of bondage in Egypt which ended with the Exodus under Moses (c.1447 B.C.). Forty years of wandering nomad life in the Sinai wilderness preceded the conquest of Caanan and its settlement by the Israelites under Joshua. Then followed three hundred twenty years during which Israel existed as a loose federation of twelve tribes who periodically united forces under a judge against an external threat. This period of history is therefore called Judges.

When King David assumed the royal leadership of Israel about 1000 B.C. there was the beginning of a shift from a nation of twelve tribes to a single tribe, Judah, as God's chosen people. Revelation became more specific as to who would serve as the faithful ones through whom Christ the Savior should come. Following David, therefore, the fortunes of the tribe of Judah became the focus of

└► cf. Gen 49

Biblical attention. The significance of the remaining tribes of Israel took on less and less importance in the unfolding of God's plan. In fact, ten northern tribes declared their independence after the death of Solomon. (931 B.C.) They became idolatrous and were decimated as a nation in the Assyrian exile (c.721 B.C.) from which they never returned in any united movement.

Yet Judah also, like the other tribes of the old nation of Israel, became less and less obedient to the will of her God, and, consequently, less fit to serve as redemptive agent. By the year 587 B.C., Judah collapsed under the onslaught of Babylon's military might, and was taken captive and exiled to Babylon. The Bible thereafter speaks of a remnant, a small group of people from the tribe of Judah who served the divine purpose of world redemption. A remnant was restored from Babylonian captivity about 537 B.C., and the worship life of God's people was restored with the rebuilding of a temple in Jerusalem. (510 B.C.) Thereafter very little is known about this remnant community except for brief periods of its history described by Ezra, Nehemiah, and Malachi. But from New Testament accounts such as the genealogy of Matthew 1, we know that the remnant group was further narrowed down till one Jewish maiden named Mary became the channel through whom the Savior of the World was born.

In Jesus Christ all the promises of salvation for the world were realized. It is He whom the long ages of recorded Biblical Revelation anticipated. Jesus Christ represented the specific, ultimate focus of all revelational light which preceded Him. By His life, death, and resurrection, salvation was accomplished for all nations. Thus the history of redemption which begins with the universal, creational activity of God, and narrows progressively till its fulfillment in Christ, becomes universal again after Christ. The concern of the Gospel, the Good News of Christ, is for every tribe, and tongue, and people, and nation,. (Rev. 5:9)

This is the pattern of revelation in the Bible. In terms of God's partners in carrying out His plan in the world the message of the Bible moves from Adam, embracing all humanity, narrows to Sethites, to Shemites, to Israelites, to Jesus Christ, and then broadens in its New Testament application to all humanity once more. Thus the Bible's message moves from the universal, becoming increasingly narrow and particular for the express purpose of redemption, becoming universal again once salvation is accomplished. The gospel of redemption in Christ is intended for the world. Look at the diagram again in the light of the forgoing observations.

## JESUS CHRIST: The Focal Point of Scripture

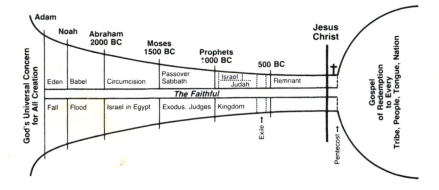

This method of diagramming the Biblical message visually emphasizes how the entire Old Testament anticipates the coming of Christ as the Messiah. The New Testament presents the Savior who lived among men, died on a cross, was buried, arose from the grave, and ascended to heaven. From the Heavenly Father's right hand He sent His Holy Spirit on Pentecost to dwell with His redeemed people which is the Church. Thereupon the Spirit-inspired Church became the carrier of the message of God's redemption for the world which had been realized in the work of the divine Son. The Church is the New Israel, called to be God's people in the world, so that God's reconciling, redeeming intention for the whole world may be fulfilled.

### Dating Revelational Epochs

An interesting observation regarding the revelational pattern described above is the apparent cycle of five hundred years between major revelational events. The events covered in Genesis 1 through 11 are impossible to date. But, beginning with Abraham, dates can be established with substantial accuracy. Abraham lived approximately 2000 B.C., Moses 1500 B.C., David 1000 B.C., the

Temple was restored after the Captivity just before 500 B.C. and Jesus was born at calendar point zero. Jesus' birth was not precisely zero in relation to our calendar, since our calendar lacks accuracy. However, His birth was within 4 to 7 years prior to point 0 in relation to our present day calendar.

The above dating can be established on the basis of Biblical references if we begin with a date of 967 B.C. for the founding of Solomon's temple. Few authorities dispute that date (plus or minus four to six years). I Kings 6:1 tells us that Solomon's temple was begun 480 years after the Exodus of the people of Israel from Egypt under Moses. Adding 480 to 967 gives us the date 1447 B.C. for the Exodus (Genesis 46:1-7). Since Moses was 80 years old when that event took place, his approximate birth year is 1527 B.C.

Exodus 12:40 observes that the length of the stay of Jacob's descendants in Egypt was 430 years. When this total is added to 1447 B.C., which was the year they left Egypt, 1877 B.C. becomes the year identifying the original move of Jacob's family from Palestine to Egypt. Since, according to Genesis 47:9, Jacob was 130 years old at the time, Jacob's birth year becomes 2007 B.C. Further, Genesis 25:26 informs us that Isaac was 60 years old when his son Jacob was born, which places Isaac's birth in the year 2067 B.C. Finally, in Genesis 21:5 we learn that Abraham was 100 years old when Isaac his son was born. Adding 100 years to the date of Isaac's birth year 2067, gives us 2167 B.C. as the birth year of Abraham. Since Abraham lived to the age of 175 years (Genesis 25:7) the year of his death is placed at 1992 B.C. by adding 175 years to the year 2167 B.C. Thus 2000 B.C. serves as a nice round figure to remember the time in Biblical history when the great patriarchs Abraham, Isaac, and Jacob were all alive. On that date Abraham was approximately 167, Isaac 67, and Jacob 15 years of age.

The dating of David's ascendancy to the royal throne simply requires adding his 40 year reign as King to the 967 B.C. date for the founding of Solomon's temple, which was the year of David's death (I Kings 2:10 & 11). The beginning date for David's reign, therefore, becomes 1007 B.C.

Restoration of the Temple after the Exile is assigned an approximate date of 500 B.C. The return from Babylon began in 537 B.C. According to the prophecy of Haggai, the building of the temple was very slow in developing, likely covering nearly two decades. The date for the restoration of temple service, therefore, approaches closely to the 500 B.C. date.

After thousands of years of anticipation and expectancy, the Seed of Promise was born. How appropriate that world history should be divided before and after His birth! Surely it was the most momentous event since creation. Jesus' life, death, and resurrection assured the restoration of unity, harmony, and fellowship between the offended God and offending humanity. The apostle Paul puts it this way:

> All this is from God, who reconciled us to Himself through Christ and gave us a ministry of reconciliation: that God was reconciling the world to Himself in Christ, not counting men's sins against them - We implore you on Christ's behalf: Be reconciled to God. God made Him who had no sin to be a sin offering for us, so that in Him we might become the righteousness of God. (I Cor. 5:18-21)

The twenty-seven books of the New Testament complete the record of the events revealed by God for the salvation of the world. The setting for the entire New Testament is the Roman world of the first century A.D. Included in the account are the Gospels which identify the major events and teachings of Jesus. Then follows the book of Acts which records the history of the growth of the Christian Church as the Good News of the realized salvation in Jesus Christ is carried to people in increasing numbers of places throughout the Roman world. The most numerous books of the New Testament are called Epistles (letters) written by various apostles to establish and regulate the life and belief of the Church. The concluding book of the Bible carries the title Revelation. It serves as a call to the Church to be faithful to her Lord as she patiently waits for a divinely established new heaven and new earth where righteousness alone will prevail.

This broad overview of the Biblical record provides a pattern which helps to identify the role particular passages play in the total message. It is so important to know when the events recorded took place, since God reveals Himself in specific times and places. History provides the setting for divine communication. In the chapters that follow, the message of the Bible will be identified in relation to specific segments of history. We shall call these historical segments revelational Epochs.

## Divine Plan Met Through Human Agents

One additional factor incorporated in the diagram reflects a very significant reality that carries through the history of redemption. A narrow channel runs through the center of the diagram from beginning to end. This is designed to portray the Biblical fact that only a small minority were really the faithful ones among those called to God's service. At any specific juncture in Bible history, the majority seemed inclined to unfaithfulness, idolatry, and falsehood. The majority were caught up in their own pursuits, their own ambitions, their personal interests and failed to find their true meaning for existence in God's service. The faithful minority alone kept their vision focused upon the realization of God's saving purposes for which they served as agency. This minority group knew the purpose of their existence and therefore lived with a sense of divine mission in their time.

To properly understand the Bible we shall have to keep three categories of people in mind. One group embraces the majority of humanity outside the circle of divine revelation, ignorant of divine truth. A second group includes those to whom the Bible's message has been made known and who have formally and externally identified themselves with it but not in a sincere, heartfelt way. They have a knowledge of the truth but deny the power of it (II Timothy 3:5). It has no impact on their lives. The third group are the Lord's faithful ones. They are not better than any others but are conscious of God's grace in their lives and live in the awareness that they are the objects of grace. These are the ones through whom the Lord's will can be brought to reality in their historical time and place. These constitute the company of the forgiven who know that the only life worth living is the life of obedient service to God. Their numbers are proportionately few. It has always been so and is to the present. But the divine plan for the ages has been and will ultimately be realized through their commitment to serving God.

## Discussion Stimulators, Chapter One

1. Why do you suppose the Bible begins with the record of the Creation of the physical world when the main purpose of Scripture is to record God's plan of salvation for the world?

2. What are some advantages of having a grasp of the larger pattern of Biblical Revelation when studying any one part of Scripture?

3. Throughout Bible history only a small minority even among the chosen people seemed to be faithful to the Lord. Do you think that is true today with those who identify themselves as Christians?

4. Through a line of faithful people, God ultimately provided Jesus as the world's Savior. They were agents or channels for fulfilling God's plan. Can Christians after Christ still serve as instruments to serve to accomplish God's plan for the world? What is that plan? How can Christians serve as partners with God to effect it?

## For Further Study:

De Graaf, S.G., *Promise and Deliverance,* (St. Catherines, Ont., Paideia Press, 1977).

Halley, H.H., *Bible Handbook,* (Grand Rapids, Zondervan, 1965) pp. 20-57.

Rhodes, A.B., *The Mighty Acts of God,* (Atlanta, John Knox Press, 1979).

Sloan, W.W., *A Survey of the Old Testament,* (Nashville, Abingdon Press, 1975).

Swiggum, H., *Bethel Series,* (Madison, WI, Adult Christian Education Foundation, 1981).

# The Nature of the Bible as Revelation

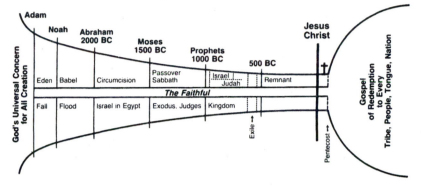

I. Defining the Terms.

II. The All-embracing Character of Revelation.

III. Divine Self-disclosure as "Word" Revelation.

    A. Creational Word.

    B. Written Word.

    C. Incarnate Word.

IV. The Bible and Revelation

V. Clarifying Statements on Revelation

VI. The Uniqueness of Biblical Revelation.

Scripture Readings
    Psalm 119:89-112.
    John
    II Peter 1:12-21.
    Romans 1:18-32.

# The Nature of the Bible as Revelation

## Defining the Terms

The word "revelation" is derived from the Latin "revelatio" whose meaning is "to unveil or uncover." It implies that something remains hidden and unknown unless it is deliberately opened to view, uncovered, so that it is no longer hidden. The words used in Scripture for revelation are the common words for "disclose," "make known," or "reveal" with a deepened meaning when applied to divine communications and their results. The most prominent word in the Old Testament is GALAH, the original meaning of which is "to be or make naked." The corresponding New Testament term is APOKALUPTO, which also signifies the removal of a veil or covering so that what is behind it or under it may be exposed to view. The predominant implication in the use of these terms is that apart from a deliberate uncovering or unveiling act, what is covered or veiled would remain hidden and, therefore, unknown.

In Biblical Theology, Revelation is seen as having both its source and its object in God. It is He who uncovers and therefore communicates knowledge concerning Himself and His will to mankind. And He does so in everything that He says and does. *Revelation is, therefore, God's sovereign initiative by which, in speech and action, He freely communicates and discloses Himself to mankind.*

Such an understanding of the nature of revelation carries with it certain implications which deserve emphasis. Revelation is a *sovereign* divine activity. There is no possible authority to which God is subject which could require Him to reveal Himself. Divine self-disclosure is initiated by God simply because He willed to do

19

so. Further, it is a *speech* and *action* revelation, a word and deed revelation embracing all that God determined to say and do. In noting that God discloses Himself *freely* the emphasis is upon the fact that revelation is a conscious, voluntary, and intentional act. God is never passive in the manifestation of Himself.

## The All-embracing Character of Revelation

Revelation embraces everything that exists. God's original act of Creation, by which the entire universe came into existence, was a revelatory act. Both the act of Creation and the cosmos which resulted tell us something about the God who made it. The Apostle Paul clearly established this in Romans 1:19 & 20:

> For what can be known about God is plain. Ever since the creation of the world, his invisible nature, namely his eternal power and deity, has been clearly perceived in the things that have been made.

Since everything we study has to do with created reality, it follows that God Himself addresses us in everything we investigate. We see evidence of His power and divine artistry everywhere. All truth is Divinely revealed truth wherever it is found, since all reality is in the grip of the Lord who holds it in its existence. Study becomes for us an act of worship. Every new discovery moves us to exclaim, "How great our God is!"

God not only disclosed Himself in Creation, He also reveals Himself and His will in a written record, the Holy Scriptures. The Bible focuses upon Divine self-disclosure that is specifically redemptive. It is a written account of the Saving acts of God in history, reconciling a lost world (cosmos) unto Himself. It is a record of God's redemptive engagement with the world as it historically unfolds. It is an account of God's saving participation in a real world of real people through whom He demonstrates His covenant faithfulness and saving intention for the world.

Beside the Revelation which comes in Creation and in the Scriptures, there is the fullest divine self-disclosure in the person of Jesus Christ. When God became incarnate in the person of His Son, the ultimate divine self-disclosure was realized. In Christ, God Himself is with us, in person, in history, participating fully with human beings on planet earth. Jesus Christ is the supreme revelational event, the fullest disclosure of the person of God in history. To really know God, therefore, we must preeminently know Jesus, personally, believingly. In Christ all revelatory events receive their real meaning in relation to God's saving purpose in history.

The above two emphases - the Bible as the record of God's saving participation in history, and Jesus Christ as a fully human, historical incarnation - sets the Christian idea of revelation apart from all other world religions. In no other "scriptures" does history assume such revelatory significance nor are there dateable incarnations in the light of which prior and subsequent history assumes its meaning.

### Divine Self-disclosure as "Word" Revelation

A repeated Biblical term used to denote God's communication of Himself is the term *Word*. Consider these examples. From the Old Testament there is Psalm 33:6, "By the word of the Lord were the heavens made and all the hosts of them by the breath of His mouth." Here the term "word" refers to the mighty act of God disclosing Himself in creation. We may call this the "Creational Word."

Then there are references such as Psalm 119:11. "Thy word have I hid in my heart that I might not sin against thee." This passage makes obvious reference to a written reservoir of truth which represents God's will for the life of the believer. It is a synonym in Psalm 119 for God's law, statutes, ordinances, and commandments, all of which has as referent a recorded account of divine interventions on behalf of God's people and His expectations for the life of His people. In this context revelation comes in the form of the Bible, or the "Written Word."

In the first chapter of the Gospel of John the term "Word" is used with reference to Jesus Christ, the supreme revelation of God to mankind. We read in verses one and fourteen,

> In the beginning was the Word, and the Word was with God, and the Word was God.

> And the Word became flesh and lived for a while among us. We have seen Hislglory, the glory of the one and only Son who came from the Father, full of grace and truth.

Here the term "word" has a very personal and specific reference to Christ as the incarnate Son of God whose coming into the world makes the heavenly Father known. (cf John 1:18) Revelation as divine self-disclosure comes to us in the person of Christ as "Incarnate Word." The word "incarnate" means "in the flesh" or "in physical form." Jesus Christ is the Word as the personal communication of God and His will.

The Biblical examples of the use of "word" in reference to divine self-disclosure in each of the above three modes could be multiplied. They are never in conflict with each other for all reveal the one God whether through the word of Creation, the word of Scripture, or the Word become flesh. The Creational Word, the Inscripturated Word, and the Incarnate Word reveal to us the God who would have remained eternally hidden and unveiled had he not sovereignly chosen to disclose Himself.

## The Bible and Revelation

The Bible is indispensible for our understanding of Revelation. It is the basic authority to which we appeal for our knowledge of God's Self-disclosure. It is a trustworthy record of the progress in history of God's revelatory acts beginning with Creation, continuing through the unfolding of the divine plan of redemption culminating in Jesus Christ, and recording the work of the Holy Spirit in the Apostolic Church. The Bible is our resource for understanding the Creational Word and for our knowledge of the Incarnate Word. The Bible clarifies our vision so that the revelation of God in the created order comes into clear focus for us. And the Bible also reveals to us Jesus Christ as the fullest revelation of God as a God of grace and salvation. The Bible, therefore, serves as our primary text. The objective of this study is to present the unity and coherence of the message of the Bible as the revelation of the redeeming God calling a lost world to Himself.

We must study the Scriptures because they provide us with knowledge of fundamental issues which we simply cannot learn from any other source. The Bible provides us with answers to what may be called ultimate questions, such as, Where did everything come from? What does it mean to be human? Is there a God? How does God relate to mankind and the world? Does historical existence have meaning? What is the ultimate purpose for which everything exists? Is there life after death? Answers to such questions are impossible to find on our own. They must be revealed to us. The Biblical answers to these questions, therefore, provide us with the Revelational Givens which serve as the presuppositions for our Christian calling in life.

The Bible is the only reliable source from which to know who God is, who we are, and the purpose, meaning, significance and goal for which everything exists. It reveals truth about mankind and his world which is available from no other source. It tells us where the world originated and where it's going, and that all of it is in the hand of the Lord who made it. It informs us that human beings are unique creatures, the crown of creation, made in the image of God. It assures us that human existence as it historically unfolds is not absurd or irrational but has inherent meaning, and is moving on to a purposeful culmination. It has one consistent message, namely, God's saving concern for a lost world. Throughout, it addresses us as human beings. The Bible speaks *about* the natural order, (sun, moon, hills, cattle, etc.) but *to* people, not only to the people who first were given the revelation, but to all people to whom the mighty acts of God are retold. We as humans are, therefore, addressed by God through the Scriptures. We are called to respond. And respond we must, either as joyful, obedient believers, or as rebelling, antagonistic unbelievers. There is no neutral third alternative.

The Bible as revelation does not come without the accompanying work of the Holy Spirit. Inspiration accompanies revelation. Revelation is God's determination to make Himself known. Inspiration is the Holy Spirit's work in the hearts and lives of those who were the original receivers of the revelation. By the inspiration of the same Holy Spirit they were moved to communicate it. The Apostle Peter puts it this way,

> For prophecy never had its origin in the will of man, but men spoke from God as they were carried along by the Holy Spirit. (II Peter 1:21)

Furthermore, this inspiration did not stop with the persons who originally received it, but carried over to their writings, the Scriptures themselves. The Apostle Paul testifies to a young pastor, Timothy, as follows:

> All Scripture is God-breathed and is useful for teaching, rebuking, correcting and training in righteousness. (II Tim. 3:16)

Finally, not only were the Biblical writers inspired by the Holy Spirit as well as the writings themselves, but those who read and study the Scriptures require the Holy Spirit's guidance to understand what is written and to respond with faith.

> We have not received the spirit of the world but the Spirit who is from God, that we may understand what God has freely given us. (I Cor. 2:12)

> The man without the Spirit does not accept the things that come from the Spirit of God, for they are foolishness to him. (I Cor. 2:14)

### Clarifying Statements on Revelation

Revelation is God's initiative by which, in speech and action, he deliberately chose to communicate and disclose Himself to mankind.

Revelation is not exhaustive. That is, it does not tell us everything about God or fully disclose Him. God always transcends the universe He created and is more than His own self-disclosure.

Revelation is addressed to human beings. God does not communicate with plants and animals in the natural order, but with people. Revelation therefore assures human beings the most noble place in reality as God-related beings, unique among the creation. It is the highest honor possible in the created order to be called into communicating fellowship with God.

Revelation as Divine self-disclosure is a comprehensive unity in all its various modes. Given by the living God in whom there can be no contradictions, Revelation contains no conflict in any of its parts.

The nature and actuality of Revelation is determined by God. He not only decided *if* He would reveal Himself but also *when, where, why, how, and to whom.* God is never under any external pressure to reveal Himself nor is He accountable to any other person or influence.

God reveals Himself personally. He is not simply an impersonal "spirit" or "positive universal influence" pervading the world. In revelation God makes Himself known and calls us to respond in an intimate, personal way to the God by whom we are addressed.

God reveals Himself generally in the created cosmos, and in the history of the nations. He reveals Himself savingly in the history of the Covenant people Israel, in Jesus Christ, and in the early New Testament Christian church.

The climax of God's self-disclosure is Jesus Christ in relation to whom all other revelational events receive their meaning. In Christ the Source and Content of revelation meet, since its source is God and its content the disclosure of the Person and Will of God. In Christ, God reveals Himself in person and His will is perfectly and finally disclosed.

The Bible is the inspired record of Divine revelation as it progressively unfolded. It is the reservoir and interpreter of revelation. It is the objective written record of the Person and Will of God.

The Holy Spirit is indispensible in the process of revelation. Not only did He inspire the authors to record the revelation so that it is perfect in its original recording, He also illuminates readers of the Scriptures, infallibly leading them to the truth, enabling believers to accept the revelation as truth and responding to it with saving faith.

The purpose of revelation is the restoration and salvation of the whole world. God's purpose is to reconcile all things unto Himself. In Christ this purpose has already been, in principle, realized. The fullest realization of God's purpose in revelation awaits the Consummation of all things at the end of time when "the kingdoms of this world will have become the Kingdom of our Lord and of His Christ, and He shall reign forever and ever." (Rev. ll:15)

## The Uniqueness of Biblical Revelation

The question of the uniqueness of Biblical Revelation may be raised at this point. Is the Bible really one of a kind with no equal or equals among the religions of the world? What about the proliferation of "scriptures" among the religions of the world? Do they not tell us something about "ultimate reality" and the moral duty of mankind? Are there not even strong parallels among the teachings of the sacred literature in the various world's religions?

A review of the writings recognized as scripture in the various world religions other than Christianity gives evidence of two broad categories of subject matter. The content of these books focus upon either myths of the gods or moral advice for mankind, or both. Consider, for example, the Vedic myths of Hinduism. Elements of nature such as the sky, the sun, and fire are deified and rituals prescribed for the veneration of the "divine" in reality. The Upanishads continue the Vedic themes, emphasizing the route a devotee must follow to reach ultimate union with the divine World

Soul. Thus, the Hindu "scriptures" emphasize the nature and characteristics of the "gods" and the appropriate relationship of human beings to these gods, to attain, finally, Ultimate Deity. An example of sacred writings where moral advice is the most prominent characteristic would be the Four Noble Truths and the Eight-Fold Pathway of Buddhism. In these there is no mention of a god or a divine spirit the existence of which is, by implication, denied. But the moral duties of mankind are spelled out in specific detail regarding human desires, speech, and conduct.

The Bible, by contrast, does not contain any myths of the gods, but rather denies the existence of any gods except the one true God who created all that exists. It then proceeds to tell us what that God has done to redeem (save) the world, including human beings, from a fallen condition. It is, therefore, an account of God's saving acts in real history to restore all things to Himself. History is the arena or setting for the saving words and deeds of the God of grace. As the inspired record of divine, saving activity in history, the Bible stands unique among religious writings. History as the setting for divine activity is either denied or unimportant in the sacred writings of other religions.

In regard to moral obligations most sacred writings present them as rules of conduct which are rewarded with benefits for this life or the life to come. Obedience to moral law is meritorious. It earns rewards. By contrast, the Bible presents salvation only by the grace of God. No amount of moral rectitude can put anyone into a favorable relation with God. No one is saved by good moral conduct. "He saved us, not because of righteous things we had done, but because of his mercy" (Titus 3:5). Obedience to the moral injunctions in the Bible is the Christian's way of expressing gratitude for the Lord's saving mercy. Good moral conduct is the believer's "thank you" for God's saving grace. Those who love God love His commandments because they are eager to please Him and to demonstrate their thankfulness through righteous living.

Further, the history of redemption as recorded in the Bible culminates in the incarnation. In the person of Jesus Christ, God has come to identify Himself with mankind on the plane of history. The Christ of the Scriptures is not, therefore, just another founder like the Buddha or Mohammed who originated religious life styles and teachings for their followers to emulate. Christ, as God's incarnate Son, is the Object of the worship and adoration of Christian believers. He is not simply the originator of a body of religious teaching which they who call themselves Christians are expected to follow. For the Christian, the primary question is not "What did Jesus teach?," but "Who is He?" For other major religions the person of the founder is less important than his teachings. For the Biblical Faith the reverse is the case. What do you think of the Christ, whose son is He?, the question Jesus posed to the disciples, (Matthew 22:43) is still the basic question of the Christian Faith. As the Incarnate Son and the resurrected, living Lord, He is the object of the worship and praise of the Christian believer. Other religious founders were simply great teachers whose teachings live on in the religious life of their followers even though, as founders, they are dead and gone.

These two factors then, identify the uniqueness of the Biblical record, namely, its character as a record of God's saving engagement with mankind in history, and its testimony to Jesus Christ as the Incarnate Son and Living Lord.

## Discussion Stimulators, Chapter Two

1. Are there some ideas, thoughts or feelings that can be communicated through actions better than through words? Why are words absolutely necessary to communicate complex ideas?

2. Can you think of several examples from the Bible in which God revealed Himself in wordless acts? Any through words alone?

3. Reflect on some reasons why the term "Word" is appropriate in reference to Jesus Christ. In this connection compare John 1:1-3 and Hebrew 1:1-3.

4. Try to image how fruitless our search for answers to "ultimate" questions would be without the revelation of the Bible.

5. Do you think people are likely to be convinced of the existence of God by studying nature alone?

6. Read a nature Psalm such as Psalm 19. What does it say about the knowledge about God reflected in nature?

7. What does the Bible reveal about human beings? What, in terms of revelation as divine communication, makes humans so special from the rest of creation?

8. Contrast obedience under pressure or threat of punishment with obedience as a response of love. Is God pleased with obedience that is motivated by fear of punishment? Is God pleased with obedience whose motivation is to earn a reward?

## For Further Study:

De Graaf, S.G., *Promise and Deliverance,* (St. Catherines, Ont., Paideia Press, 1977) I, pp. 17-26.

Henry, C. F., *Revelation and the Bible,* (Grand Rapids, Baker, 1958).

Murray, J., *Calvin on Scripture and Divine Sovereignty,* (Grand Rapids, Bakers, 1960).

Vos, Gerhardus, *Biblical Theology,* (Grand Rapids, Eerdmans, 1948) Part 1, Chapters 1 & 2.

Warfield, B.B., *The Inspiration and Authority of the Bible,* (Phila., Presbyterian and Reformed Press, 1948).

# CHAPTER THREE

## Adamic Epoch of Biblical Revelation

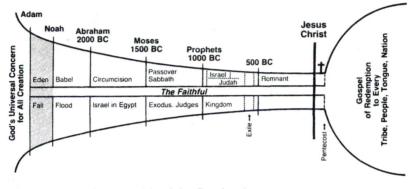

I. The Essentials of the Creation Account.

II. Pre-redemptive Biblical Revelation.

III. Redemptive Biblical Revelation.

    A. The Garden Theme--Fall and Restoration.

    B. Divine Solution for Human Evil.

Scripture Readings
    Genesis 1-3
    Psalm 8
    Psalm 19
    Psalm 29
    Psalm 65
    Psalm 104
    Psalm 147
    Romans 5
    I Corinthians 15:35-38
    Ephesians 5:6-9

# Adamic Epoch
# of Biblical Revelation

WITHIN the general pattern of Biblical Revelation there are also discernable Revelational Periods or Epochs. These Epochs are identified with specific persons and events through whom and through which God revealed Himself. The revelatory engagement initiating each epoch sets the pattern for divine-human encounter for the specific historical era which follows, till a new epoch begins. The major epochs of Biblical Revelation are the Adamic, Noahic, Abrahamic, Mosaic, Prophetic, and Apostolic.

The Biblical account of God's self-disclosure during the Adamic Epoch must be divided into two parts. The Bible records divine communication before the advent of sin into the human experience and after that world shaking event. We shall use the term Pre-redemptive Revelation for the former and Redemptive Revelation for the latter. The term "Pre-Redemptive Revelation" refers to Genesis 1 & 2 which records the Creation account and God's dealings with Adam, representing the human race, before the Fall. The term , therefore, identifies the Biblical record of divine revelation before it was necessary to redeem mankind and the world from a fallen, lost condition. "Redemptive Revelation" covers everything else in the Bible from Genesis 3 onward as the record of God's unfolding plan to save the world from its sinfully flawed condition.

## The Essentials of The Creation Account

The Biblical account of Creation (Genesis 1) has probably been subjected to a greater variety of interpretations than any other part of Scripture. Most disagreements revolve around the "when" and "how" of creation, or the age of the earth and the length of the creation "days." These issues will probably never be resolved to the unanimous satisfaction of sincere Bible students. There are, however, several matters of crucial significance in the Creation account which must be affirmed without reservation if we are faithful to Scripture. They provide the basis for all God's dealings with the world and mankind in the message of the rest of Scripture. Throughout the Bible the sovereign Creator is the God whose providence overrules world history and whose love for the world He created motivated His saving concern for it.

These unavoidable conclusions are drawn from the Bible's Creation story:

1. Creation is solely by God's initiative. He alone created the universe and everything in it. The divine activity stands out with unmistakable boldness. The word "God" appears thirty-two times in the creation account. He "created," "said," "saw," "divided," "called," "made," "set," and "blessed."

2. Creation is by divine fiat. God spoke and all the substance which makes up the universe came into existence. He alone was the pre-existent eternal One. Nothing else shares His eternality. Everything else partakes of created finitude and is dependent for its continued existence on the God who made it.

3. God created as an act of His will, not out of necessity. Nothing outside of His own being compelled His creating activity. God is free in the exercise of His will and under no compulsion.

4. God created everything good in its beauty, order, and design. The problem of evil may not be resolved by recourse to God as its source.

5. Genesis 1-3 is not a scientific, sequential historical record. However, the events recorded are accepted in the rest of the Bible as real, historical time-bound events. References to these chapters in the prophetic and apostolic writings are to actual persons and events.

6. God provided everything necessary for a fulfilling, purposeful existence for human life. This provision included the possibility of fellowship with God, supportive companionship with people (husband, wife, children, others), and a wholesome, natural environment to sustain life.

The special role that human beings were assigned in created reality is recognized in Genesis Chapter Two. Adam was a communicating partner with God. They talked to each other as personal companions. God conversed with Adam, but not with trees, or animals, or any other part of non-human natural reality. The implication is that human beings are privileged to communicate directly with the Creator. This consciousness of a fellowshipping relationship with God identifies the unique, privileged role that humans fill in the created order.

With this privileged position came an associated responsibility. Human beings were created to be ruling stewards of the created world, responsible before God for its care and development. The divine intent of Creation was that all reality should reflect the glory of the One who created it. The purpose for which the whole Creation existed was to reflect with honoring credit upon its Maker. As ruling stewards, the purpose for which humans were created was to serve as spokespersons for Creation. Plants and hills, stars and rivers can't talk. Humans would speak for them. Vegetation and animals can't think rationally. Humans would think for them. Non-human things can't consciously and intentionally praise and worship their Creator. Humans must do this on behalf of non-human reality.

The natural world reflects God's glory passively, like a mirror reflects the image of a person, or a painting reflects the skill and intelligence of an artist. But people, created in God's image, can willingly, consciously, and deliberately honor the Creator and "talk of all his wonderful acts" (Psalm 105:2). Of course, since humans are not passive in their God-relatedness, they can and do consciously and deliberately rebel against God and dishonor Him, which a passive natural world cannot do. The purpose of human life was not intended as a self-centered existence exploiting the natural world for its own selfish interest. Rather, its purpose was the care and development of creation's resources as worshipful tribute to the God who called it into existence. The best welfare of human life was able to be served only in the consciousness of responsibility to God for whom all things ultimately existed. It was God's world whose care was entrusted to human minds and hands.

### Pre-redemptive Biblical Revelation

Genesis 2:8-25 records God's provision of a garden as a place of habitation for humans (Adam and Eve). Everything necessary for a fulfilling human existence in fellowship with God was present. Focusing particularly on Genesis 2:15-17, three symbols emerge which are instructive for our understanding of pre-Fall Revelation. They are the symbols of the Garden, of Work, and of a Tree.

The Garden symbolizes a place of fellowship with God. It is not in the first instance an abode for mankind as such, but a place of reception of man into fellowship with God. It represents a place where mankind can live the God-centered, God-related life for which he was called into existence. God dwells in the garden with His presence in order to make it possible for humans to dwell with their Maker.

Work symbolizes God's intention that mankind be engaged in creative, fulfilling, purposeful activity. The work intended includes both physical and intellectual activity. Verse 15 mentions that God placed man in the garden "to till it and keep it." He was expected, by useful labor, to be God's assigned custodian of the earth to develop its productive capacity. Work as intellectual activity is suggested in Genesis 2:19 & 20 where Adam is given responsibility to "name" the animal kingdom. "Naming" means far more than assigning an identifying label. Rather it implies the recognition of the unique character of each animal and the specific role each of the various animals fills in God's design for life. Mankind was thus assigned the task as ruling steward of the creation on behalf of God and accountable to God.

The third of the symbols for our understanding of pre-Fall revelation is that of the "tree of the knowledge of good and evil" (verse 17). Unlike the other trees in the garden of God/human fellowship, this tree was not to be used for the nourishment of human life. It served as the test of human willingness to live in obedience to the Creator upon whom they were dependent. The intent was to lead man through a period of probation to the state of religious maturity, to the level of pure delight in obedience to God and the enjoyment of His fellowship. Perfect human fulfillment was possible only in an obedient relationship with God.

The first two chapters of Genesis present us with the divinely provided condition for the ideal, happy human existence. This perfect condition included intimate companionship with God, fulfilling, purposeful activity in the form of creative work, and obedience to the God whose perfect will established the pattern of life that would enrich human existence and glorify the Creator.

### Redemptive Biblical Revelation

Humans, created as God's ruling stewards of the creation, chose instead to declare their independence from God, distorting the purpose for which they and all creation existed, requiring God's saving intervention in history.

The essence of the Fall is seen in mankind's refusal to live in obedient dependence upon God. It consists in the refusal to respond to God as God's spokesman for the creation to bring it to the fulfillment of its potential in praise of the Creator. Man declared his independence, and proceeded to attempt to deify himself, to make himself the center of the creation, exchanging dependency upon God for dependency on evil. The Fall consists, therefore, in mankind's determination to make themselves the center of reality in place of God, a declaration of independence from their Maker. It represents a rejection of God-centeredness as the proper life direction with man-centeredness. It consists in an attempt to find fulfillment within the limits of human resources, rather than in a relation to God. It is the essence of humanism. All the resources of nature were enlisted in the service of human self gratification instead of God glorification.

Genesis 3:1-6 describes the Devil's technique in tempting humans away from dependence upon and responsibility to God. Satan subtly appeals to three areas of human vulnerability to temptation, three dimensions of human personality which are sensitive to destructive responses. In I John 2:15 & 16 the Apostle identifies this vulnerability in terms of lust. Lust as self-destructive human craving has three forms, namely, fleshly lust, visual lust, and prideful lust. As the Apostle puts it, "whatever is not of the Father is of the world, the lust of the flesh, the lust of the eyes, and the pride of life."(KJV) The demonic strategy was to attack these three human vulnerabilities in order to redirect life's purpose away from seeking a relationship with God as highest goal and toward self-gratification.

The specific approach involved in this Satanic temptation are evident in Genesis 3:6:

> Fleshly lust, "good for food."
>
> Visual lust, "pleasant to the eyes."
>
> Prideful lust, "desired to make one wise."

This "fall" of humanity from the lofty position as God's ruling steward of creation brought all creation down with it. Creation no longer had a God-respondent being able to direct its chorus of praise to the Creator. The principle of death, essentially a relation of brokenness between God and the entire creation, prevailed. This principle of death reigned supreme until the coming of Jesus Christ, the Second Adam, who came "not to do my own will but the will of Him who sent me" (John 6:38). Christ, in perfect obedience to and dependence upon the Father, was also attacked by the Devil in a three-fold temptation (Luke 4:1-13). Careful study of that event reveals that the Devil's strategy in approaching Christ followed the same pattern as the original temptation in Eden. He attacked the same three areas of human vulnerability. But where Adam and Eve failed, Christ prevailed. He, therefore, perfectly qualified for the role as Second Adam, the true and perfect representative human. As such, mankind may be restored to true God-relatedness through identification with Jesus Christ. "For as in Adam all die, so all in Christ will be made alive." (I Cor. 15:22)

### Garden Theme - Fall and Restoration

The relationship of the Fall to the rest of the Bible's message may be clarified by tracing the garden symbolism in the Scriptures. Human beings, as divine image bearers, were created to live in covenant fellowship with their God. A garden was prepared by God as the context for this happy Divine/human fellowship. God was man's friend. They walked together as Friend with friend in unity and peace.

But then came the *Fall*. Falling for the Devil's lie, the original humans declared their independence from God. They broke covenant. The God/man relationship was shattered. They, therefore, *had* to be evicted from the garden. There was no place remaining for Creator/created harmony and peace. The Great Divorce had taken place and eviction from the garden was an unavoidable consequence.

The rest of the Bible, after the event of the Fall, recounts for us what God determined to do, in His mercy and grace, to right the wrong of man's corrupting rebellion. Accordingly, there are repeated anticipations of the restoration of fellowship with God under the symbol of restored gardens. Psalm 23 describes a garden scene, with green pastures and quiet waters, where the Shepherd will restore the soul. Ezekiel 36:35 speaks God's word of promise to the restored exiles that the "land that was laid waste will become like the garden of Eden." Isaiah 65:25 uses "garden" language to describe the ultimate place of fellowship God will provide, where "the wolf and lamb will feed together - they will not harm nor destroy in all my holy mountain."

To restore mankind to fellowship with God, the Divine Son had to endure agony in a garden called Gethsemane. (Matthew 26:36-46) Jesus had to experience the alienation from the Heavenly Father that the sin in the first garden caused. Jesus went to the garden craving fellowship with His heavenly Father. He prayed a heart-wrenching prayer: "Father, don't forsake me now. Let this cup pass, for to drink it I'll have to cry 'My God, my God, why have you forsaken me!' To live apart from you is death. Don't leave me now."

Gethsemane was the second Eden. The Second Adam in the second Eden endured the consequent rejection of the Father that the sin in the first Eden caused. But Gethesemane is also the reverse of Eden. In the first Eden, Adam forsook God, and God had to evict him from the garden, for fellowship was broken. In Gethsemane, God forsook the God/man, the second Adam, and man, in the form of an unbelieving mob, evicted the Divine Son from the garden. It had to be. He who bore man's sin must bear its penalty, alienation from God, eviction from a garden of fellowship. There was no other way to restore the broken relationship.

And, like the first Eden, there was temptation in Gethsemane, too. Jesus was tempted to avoid the cross, tempted to move contrary to the Father's will. The perfect representative man knew well the power of temptation even as He spoke to His garden companions, "Pray that you do not enter into temptation." (Matthew 26:41) Jesus did not yield to temptation as Adam had done, but went willingly to the cross.

The "garden" theme of Scripture continues following the crucifixion since Jesus was buried in a garden, a garden from which he triumphantly arose. "Death could not hold its prey." He arose. The resurrection garden assured the restoration of fellowship between the offended Lord and His offending people. In the resurrection garden the heavenly Father placed the stamp of divine approval upon the Savior's work of redemption. So that, "If you confess with your mouth Jesus as Lord, and believe in your heart that God raised Him from the dead, you will be saved." (Romans 10:9)

The Covenant Mediator has restored covenant fellowship for His covenant people, because, where Adam failed, Christ prevailed. Where the first Adam failed, Jesus prevailed.

The Bible closes with a description of a garden scene in the very last chapter of Revelation. Like the first garden in Scripture (Eden) it is God who provides it; but unlike Eden, nothing impure will ever enter it, nor anyone who does what is shameful or deceitful. And there will be no more curse, no more demonic temptation, no more Fall.

The heavenly garden includes a "river of the water of life, flowing from the throne of God and of the Lamb" and "the tree of life yielding its fruit, whose leaves are for the healing of the nations." The throne of God and of the Lamb will be there and "His servants will serve Him. They shall see His face and His name will be on their foreheads - And they will reign forever and ever." (Revelation 22:1-5)

### Divine Solution for Human Evil

God's response to the Fall is recorded in Genesis 3:14-21. It introduces the redeeming act on the part of God by which He provides a gracious solution to human rebellion. This is not God's initial act of *grace* after the Fall, which is indicated already in Genesis 3:8-13 describing God's search for fallen mankind. God graciously and mercifully took the initiative to call fallen mankind back to Himself. There was neither desire nor capability for human initiative to restore the relationship. If fellowship was to be restored, it had to begin with God's side. And it was.

Genesis 3:14-21 is the first revelation of the shape of the program of redemption, namely, the defeat of the kingdom of darkness through a righteous SEED, or offspring, or descendant of mother Eve. Someone born of a woman would eventually right the wrong of human corruption.

In this passage, the serpent represents all that is opposed to God, the demonic forces which tempt humans away from a life of joyful obedience to the Lord. In verse 14 God pronounces a curse upon the demonic forces which oppose Him. Verse 15 elaborates this pronouncement by indicating how the final victory of divine salvation over the kingdom of evil will be accomplished.

> And I will put enmity between you (Satan) and the woman (Eve), and between your offspring and hers; he will crush your head and you will strike his heel.

Sometimes called the "Mother Promise," this divine strategy includes two major elements, namely, conflict and victory.

*Conflict.*

Genesis 3:15 anticipates an extended period of human history during which those loyal to the Lord and those loyal to the Evil One will be in perpetual conflict. The offspring of the serpent refers to unbelieving followers of the Devil, and Eve's offspring represents those who are true to the Lord. This is the only Biblically significant distinction of the human family, believers and unbelievers, faithful to the covenants of promise, and unfaithful. All other distinctions are insignificant whether racial, national, color, or economic which existentially appear to be so significant in human relations. Unity of faith in the redeeming God should bridge all other external distinctions, producing a communion of saints distinguished from the category of humans identified with the works of darkness.

*Victory.*

Ultimately the conflict involves a person (he) and the Devil (you). The "he" who will crush the head of the serpent anticipates the final victory of Christ at the Cross of Calvary. There Jesus Christ struck the fatal, head crushing blow to the power of evil, to assure victory of the divine plan of salvation. "You will strike his heel" assures the painful, though not fatal, injury to the Savior that demonic power would inflict. Thus, this first prophecy of the plan of salvation provides a vague, general outline of what is to follow in the message of the Scriptures. The fulfillment of the prophecy would not be realized completely until Christ, the ultimate *"Offspring"* of the woman, destroyed the works of the Devil at great cost and injury to Himself at the cross.

While the fullest meaning of the "offspring of the woman" is a reference to Jesus Christ, the term has a broader meaning as well. It has the meaning of "descendants who serve God's purposes in the world." Similarly, "offspring of the serpent" refers to human descendants who serve as agents of Evil.

Throughout the Bible there are references to descendants who serve as agents for God's purposes. Some of these references should be noted.

**Noah.** Genesis 9:9 "I now establish my covenant with you and with your descendants after you."

**Abraham.** Genesis 17:7 "I will establish my covenant between me and you and your descendants after you for the generations to come, to be your God and the God of your descendants after you."

**Israel.** Deuteronomy 10:15 "Yet the Lord set His affection on your forefathers and loved them, and He chose you, their descendants, above all the nations."

**David.** Psalm 89:3 & 4a "You said, I have made a covenant with my chosen one, I have sworn to David my servant, I will establish your line (descendants) forever."

**A Savior as THE offspring.** Galations 3:16 "The promises were spoken to Abraham and to his seed (offspring). The Scripture does not say "seeds" meaning many people, but "and to your seed," meaning one person, who is Christ."

**Believers as offspring.** Galations 3:29 "If you belong to Christ, then you are Abraham's seed and heirs according to the promise."

## *Consequences of the Fall*

The repercussions of the Fall in the life of humanity are summarized in Genesis 3:17-21. The Lord addressed Eve, as verse 16 records it, by observing two matters which would burden her life. They included painful child bearing and subordination to male authority. The first of these is too narrowly restricted to the physical pain of delivery. It also includes the painful stress, worry, concern, and disappointment that raising children entails. Parent/children conflicts are sin-caused and were not intended in the original, perfect state. The second, female subordination to male domination, is also a sin-caused condition from which liberation is only possible as a fruit of redemption. Only in redeemed relationships is true equality of dignity restored, where men and women relate in mutually enriching roles as God has prescribed. Political action programs toward liberation will always fall short of that which can be accomplished only through the reborn life of faith.

The consequences for Adam and all creation are implied in verses 17-19. Adam received his sentence as one who shared with Eve the mutual guilt of disobedience. There is no basis for establishing greater or lesser guilt. They were "one flesh" and as such fell together. The curse of "painful toil" rested upon both of them. Work was originally intended by the Creator to be creative and fulfilling whether physical or intellectual. Post-fall work takes on the labor image, frustrating, monotonous, unfulfilling. Nature itself became a hindrance in its corrupted condition. "It will produce thorns and thistles for you" (verse 18). Only redeemed work, reordered toward the honor of the Lord, escapes the dead hand of ultimate uselessness.

Remember, as a married couple, one flesh, representing the whole human family, they fell. Therefore, men share the consequences of pain and disappointment that bearing children entails, and women share the futility and drudgery that ultimately useless labor entails. But living in restored fellowship with the Lord can make family relations joyful and work humanly enriching and God glorifying.

God's gracious provision of a covering for his fallen image bearers is recorded in verse 21. The life of innocent animal victims had to be sacrificed to make the leather (skin) clothing. The general, loving concern of God to make provision for a disobedient mankind is the primary implication. Redemption through shed blood is also suggested although the Biblical theme of atonement through sacrifice is clarified specifically later (Genesis 15).

## Conclusion

We do not know, and the Bible gives us no basis for determining, how much of an historical time-lapse there was during the Adamic Epoch. When the Bible is silent, we must conclude that God has sovereignly determined not to satisfy our curiosity in the matter. Genesis 5 cannot be used to count back to a specific date for the beginning of human life since Hebraic genealogies tend to be restricted to prominent persons only, not every single intervening generation.

However long the Adamic epoch lasted, this much is sure. Those who were faithful to the Lord lived by the promise that God would bring salvation to a fallen world through His own design and plan. That plan would include the eventual destruction of the kingdom of evil through One born of a woman. The life of faith encouraged from one generation to the next rested upon the promise of God who would not allow the total corruption of His once beautiful creation. Believers lived in hope, a hope that rested in the faithful promise of God Himself.

**Discussion Stimulators, Chapter Three**

1. Review the essential truths that are emphasized in the Creation account from Genesis 1. Do you think it is spiritually profitable to emphasize aspects of the Creation event beyond these essential factors?

2. A "steward" is a person who is entrusted with the care and keeping of the properties owned by another. What are some ways in which human beings can fulfill their calling to be stewards of God's world?

3. What makes work satisfying and fulfilling or the opposite? Can any type of work or employment be done in a manner which honors the Lord? How does one gain a sense of purpose and meaning in daily work?

4. Reflect upon the concept of sin as a declaration of independence from God.

5. Lust is soul-destroying craving, or self-destructive desires. Can you identify some fleshly, visual, and prideful cravings that are self-destructive? By contrast, what desires are physically and spiritually wholesome and enriching? See I Corinthians 14:1.

6. The Bible is an optimistic Book because it assures us that God has triumphed over evil. How should this affect the way Christians relate to the struggle between good and evil in this world?

**For Further Study:**

De Graaf, S.G., *Promise and Deliverance*, (St. Catherines, Ont., Paideia Press, 1977) I, pp. 29-55.

Everest, F.A., *Modern Science and the Christian Faith* (Wheaton, Van Kampen Press, 1948).

Lewis, C.S., *The Great Divorce* (New York, Macmillan, 1971).

Vos, G., *Biblical Theology* (Grand Rapids, Eerdmans, 1948) Part I, Chapters 3 & 4.

Wright, G.E., *Biblical Archaeology,* (Philadelphia, Westminster Press, 1960), Chapter 1.

# CHAPTER FOUR

# *Noahic Epoch of Biblical Revelation*

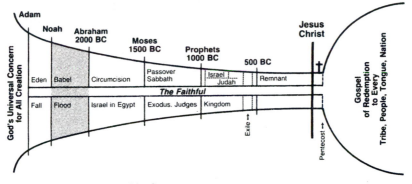

I. The Noahic Covenant.

    A. Parties to the Covenant.

    B. Obligations of the Covenant.

    C. Confirming Sign of the Covenant.

II. The Extent of the Flood.

III. Other Flood Traditions.

IV. The Tower of Babel.

Scripture Readings
    Genesis 6-11
    Matthew 24:36-51
    Luke 17:20-37
    I Peter 3:8-22

# Noahic Epoch
# of Biblical Revelation

AFTER the Fall, the Bible tells us that evil became increasingly extensive in the human family. By the time of Noah, which may have been untold millennia since Adam, just one family, Noah's own, is recorded as living in righteousness before God. The judgment of the Lord in the form of a massive Flood was poured out upon the unbelieving world. But Noah and his family were saved so that they and their faithful descendants could serve as God's obedient agents for realizing the continuation of the plan of redemption.

There is a rhythm or pattern present in Genesis following the Creation account and leading up to the account of the Flood. Notice the progression in the Bible's record.

| | |
|---|---|
| God creates a perfect order | Genesis 1 & 2 |
| Man falls, producing corruption | Genesis 3:1-7 |
| God graciously intervenes (Mother Promise) | Genesis 3:8-24 |
| Man's corruption increases | Genesis 4-6:12 |
| God graciously intervenes (Flood) | Genesis 6:13-10:32 |
| Man's corruption becomes pervasive | Genesis 11 |
| God graciously intervenes (Call of Abraham) | Genesis 12-25 |

The "rhythm" pattern helps emphasize the Flood as primarily an act of Grace and secondarily an act of judgment. The salvation of the world was contingent on the preservation of a people who would serve as agents for fulfilling God's redemptive plan. Those unwilling to serve, who threaten to extinguish the faithful line, must go. So, Noah and his family were *not* saved as a reward for their righteousness, but because they alone lived in obedience to the Lord and, therefore, could serve as agents for God's redeeming purposes in history.

A summary of chapters four to nine of Genesis demonstrates this "rhythm" pattern of human failings and divine interventions to sustain God's plan of redemption.

*Genesis four.*

Conflict, jealousy, and murder indicate convincingly the consequences of the Fall in the lives of Adam's descendants (verses 1-16). Even though great advances are made in the areas of husbandry (verse 20), the fine arts (verse 21), and manufacturing (verse 22), all human effort ends in futility apart from a right relation with God (verses 23 & 24). But God will provide a people of His choosing, descendants of Seth, who will be the channel of Salvation. They will continue a faithful minority line for God's service, a worshipping community of faith who will "call upon the name of the Lord."

*Genesis five.*

The line of promise is identified from Adam to Noah, but the principle of death, a consequence of sin, is monotonously emphasized by the repetition "and he died."

*Genesis 6:1-7.*

The spiritual decline of mankind reached such proportions that divine intervention was necessary to prevent the total disappearance of a righteous people through whom God's redeeming design for the world could be continued. Note especially how verse 5 describes the pervasiveness of evil:

Intensity and extent: "how great on earth."

Inward corruption: "every inclination of thought."

Absoluteness: "his heart was only evil."

Habitualness: "all the time."

*Genesis 6:8 to Genesis 9.*

Here we have the account of the Flood as God's judgment on the unbelieving "offspring of the serpent" and His preservation of the righteous, "offspring of the woman." With these, the Lord covenants to continue the grand design to save the world. They are the privileged agents through whom the plan of redemption can be implemented.

### The Noahic Covenant

The Biblical term for the gracious relationship between God and humanity is "covenant." It denotes a relationship between covenanting partners, based on stipulated promises or obligations, and confirmed with a sign or reminder of their commitment. Already in the God/Adam relationship the elements of covenant were present. God, party of the first part, and Adam, party of the second part, entered upon an agreement requiring obligations from both sides and confirmed with a sign or reminder of a continuing loyalty (the tree in the garden). Adam failed to meet his part of the agreement, obedience. God remained faithful and continued to pursue mankind, graciously calling humanity back to a renewed relationship.

With Noah representing the human family we have God renewing covenant to continue His relationship of saving grace with the world. Genesis 9:8-17 records this covenant renewal episode. God initiated the relationship and invited Noah, his family, and all living beings into fellowship with Himself. God's obligations included the promise to preserve the world from ever experiencing such a devastating flood disaster again. Noah, as representative of mankind and his world, obligates himself to obedience to his Maker. The obedience required is spelled out in verses 1-7 of Genesis 9. Noah must be fruitful and multiply, serve as caretaking steward of animal and plant kingdoms and regard as precious all forms of life, especially human life which bore the stamp of the divine image.

The sign or formal reminder of this covenant relationship was the rainbow. A natural phenomenon like the rainbow was so appropriate as a sign at this juncture in redemptive history. It follows a natural catastrophe, the flood, and concerns the broader natural context since the covenant embraces "all living creatures of every kind." It is no wonder that some theologies identify the Noahic Covenant as the Covenant of Nature. Such terminology is permissable so long as it does not imply a distinctive agreement separate from God's approach to mankind before and after this episode. The Bible is a single covenant document. It records God's gracious dealings with a fallen humanity and world in order to restore and redeem it. Noah, as Adam long before him and many others to follow, was a representative for the human side of this historically unfolding covenant drama. Repeatedly, reference is made to an "everlasting covenant." The term "everlasting" does not allow for a brief, historically terminated relationship. Though the human side of the agreement repeatedly failed, God's faithfulness is the ultimate guarantee of a relationship that will ever-last.

   The rainbow stands then as a reminder to people of all generations of their responsibility before God to care for and bring to fruition the natural potential of creation. For God, every rainbow is a reminder of His promise to preserve the natural order from ever again enduring a destructive flood of such catastrophic dimensions. God has kept His word. Noah led the way for humans to break theirs since he proceeded to misuse the fruit of a vineyard for gluttonous self-indulgence (Genesis 9:20-21). Thus he misused the natural resources which he, as a steward responsible to God, was assigned to preserve and care for.

### Extent of the Flood

There is a great deal of dispute among Bible scholars as to whether the Flood was universal, covering the entire planet, or local, covering a specific geographical area. Even archaeologists debate the evidence for an ancient flood in the Mesopotamian region and its possible relation to the Bible's account. C. Leonard Wooley's book *Ur of the Chaldees* is very intriguing. Though he does not claim archaeological evidence for the Noahic Flood, he recounts the discovery in south Mesopotamia of a massive sedimentary layer of fine, even-textured clay silt, over eight feet thick, deposited in one settling of waters. There were no layers which would have indicated repeated, smaller inundations like rivers overflowing their banks in successive intervals. Calculations of the amount of water required to deposit so thick a sedimentary layer indicate a body of water covering the entire Mesopotamian Valley, four hundred miles north to south and one hundred miles east to west. Such a massive flood would inundate all human civilization in that part of the world, bringing it to an abrupt end, an occurrence to which archaeology attests during the 4th millenium B.C.

Supporters of a universal flood theory point out the inclusive nature of the language used in the Genesis account, such as, "waters over the whole earth," and "every creature under heaven." Further, while there may not be thick sedimentary deposits in other places similar to that found in Mesopotamia, other evidences suggest the presence of deep waters in unexpected places in the world. Universal waters may explain the glaciers, skeletons of sea animals far inland on several continents, and geologic formations requiring massive force to shape. And, finally, failure to take the account of the Flood in the literal sense of the terminology employed seems to some to call into question the trustworthiness of the Bible.

Those who would advance a localized flood as the intention of the Biblical account observe that the events recorded are seen from the point of view of an eye-witness. The inclusive terminology must be understood from the vantage point of someone present on the scene. Thus, references to "every living thing that moved on the earth perished," "the waters flooded the earth," and all other inclusive terminology must be understood from the point of view of Noah as observer. From his point of view, everything was covered and perished. This is not unusual in the Bible. Consider Luke 2:1 where a decree is mentioned that all the inhabited world must be taxed. The reference is, of course, to the Roman Empire world, the "world" of Luke's readers, not to the Mayan civilization of Central America or any other civilization which existed also at that time.

The local flood position also helps to understand how a ship three hundred feet long could hold all the varieties of animals necessary to assure their survival. Only those species indigenous to the Mesopotamian Valley had to be spared from extinction. Not elephants (Africa and India) or giraffes (Africa) or polar bears (North America) or kangaroos (Australia).

The controversy surrounding the universal flood/local flood dialogue runs the risk of distracting attention from the real issue. That issue is the place of the Flood event in the history of redemption. Noah and those with whom he shared ethnic identity were called to be God's faithful covenant people. They were the descendants of Adam's son Seth who were chosen to serve as agents through whom God's saving concern for the world could be realized. Sethites were the chosen bearers of revelation and salvation. The salvation of the world was contingent on their willingness to be a people of God's choosing to do God's work in the world. When the vast majority of these Sethites refused, God had to come in judgment on them for the sake of the world. With the privilege of partnership with God came a responsibility which they shirked. Other humans living outside Mesopotamia, descendants of Adam's other children, were not covenant people and did not have to be destroyed. The redemptive purpose of God in history did not hinge on their faithfulness. But the Sethite people had to go, except for Noah's faithful family, so God could begin anew to preserve an obedient people of His choosing through whom the plan of salvation could continue.

## Other Flood Traditions

There are many ancient flood accounts in addition to the one recorded in the Bible. Nearly every major ancient civilization had one. An example would be one such as the Gilgamesh Epic which is of Sumerian origin and probably pre-dates the Biblical recording of the Noahic Flood. Similarities and differences between the two accounts are listed by Merrill F. Unger *Archaeology and the Bible* and may be summarized as follows:

> The Flood is divinely planned in both.
>
> Both indicate a divine relation to a hero in the story.
>
> Both relate the flood to human moral defection.
>
> In both, the hero, his relatives and animals are spared.
>
> Both include divine instruction to build a huge ship.
>
> Both describe a devastating natural calamity.
>
> Both indicate a specific time duration for the event.
>
> Both identify the ship's landing place.
>
> Each recounts the sending of birds to determine whether the waters had receded.
>
> Both describe acts of worship after the deliverance.
>
> Both allude to special blessings on the hero of the account.

Substantial differences exist between the two accounts also. The following should be noted:

> There are significant durational disagreements regarding the length of the flood, Gilgamesh about 14 days, Noah's 150 days.

> Many people assist Utnapishtim to build in the Gilgamesh Epic while Noah is ridiculed by his contemporaries.

> The Genesis account includes only what an eyewitness could experience and observe, and reflects an authentic daily log of such a witness.

> Gilgamesh (and all other non-Biblical accounts) includes details beyond the ability of an observer to notice. It, therefore, partakes of the nature of myth.

> In Gilgamesh, the hero, Utnapishtim, becomes a god, as does his wife also, a typical Primitist concept of outstanding humans attaining to deity. Noah remains human, subject to human weaknesses (drunkenness), requiring divine forgiveness.

> In the Gilgamesh Epic, there is no promise or covenant assuring non-recurrence of such a catastrophic flood.

The original flood event apparently served as the source of all later accounts. Generations of oral tradition kept the event before the consciousness of people for centuries. Some distortion of the original facts undoubtedly occurred as the story was repeated from one generation to the next. By the time it was committed to written form these distortions were permanently recorded in most cases. Our faith in the inspired reliability of the Bible leads us to affirm the Genesis account as the true standard by which to judge the truth or error of all others.

After the Flood, Noah's descendants proceeded to increase in number. In the process another long period of decline was inaugurated requiring God to intervene to make certain His plan of redemption proceeded on schedule. God called Abraham to leave his pagan associations in Ur and move to a "promised land" where he and his descendants were to live as God's faithful people. Genesis 11:10-32 summarizes revelation history from the time of Noah leading up to the reestablishment of God's covenant with

Abraham. The movement of redemptive revelation is from a broadly universal reference to Noah and the natural order, then the Nations and their scattering, until Abraham becomes the chosen channel of revelation. At this point redemption history narrows in its focus to one Patriarchal Family, that of Abraham.

## The Tower of Babel

The period between the Flood and Abraham includes the Tower of Babel episode (Genesis 11:1-9). Babel represents united opposition against God, and demonstrates the confusion and anarchy in human affairs that result when God's will for life is rejected.

The Tower was probably a Ziggurat, a pagan temple tower, quite common in the ancient Middle East. Excavations at Ur revealed three built in successive stages on the same spot. The last one was built by the Chaldeans in the eighth century. Hence, the designation "of the Chaldeans" is a later addition by a copiest to identify the place geographically for readers after the Chaldean era. The Ziggurat was built in progressively smaller sections one on top of the other in pyramid form. The massive lower level, colored dark gray, represented the underworld. The next level, colored light orange, represented the inhabited earth. Next came a blue colored section representing the sky or natural heavens. The topmost structure was gold which represented heaven itself. Here sacrifices and worship ritual were offered to the moon-god. Thus the temple tower was a microcosm of a pagan cosmology or view of the universe, a four stage representation that reached "to the heavens." Its construction, therefore, was an act of rebellion against God and a substitution of false religion in place of His service.

This false religion with its temple tower was designed to provide the security of a "name" or reputation or purposeful existence apart from God. It further identifies the unwillingness of humans to fulfill their God-given mandate to fill the earth and develop its resources in praise to the Creator. The Babel episode reveals the essence of all false religion. The word "religion" etymologically comes from the Latin "religare" which means "to tie together or reconnect." One's religion is that which ties the loose ends of life together providing the value which assures that life is worth living. That which provides a sense of meaning, purpose, and coherence to life is one's religion. Everyone has a religion in this root sense.

Unfortunately, any religion for which God is not the unifying center, the One who gives meaning to human existence, ends in Babel confusion.

The Tower of Babel represents the continuing fruitless human attempt to find purpose in life apart from God. Its effort was to establish successful life relationships in which God had no place, which is the essence of humanism. Even after the scattering of the peoples to diffuse the rebellion against God, the vain human pursuit continued. Right up to the time of Terah, Abraham's father who served strange gods, the effort continued. Clearly the necessity for divine intervention to assure the success of God's plan of salvation had come again. This He did in a renewed revelational approach through Abraham.

## Discussion Stimulators, Chapter Four

1. The Flood was an act both of divine judgment on an unbelieving world and an act of grace in the preservation of Noah and his family. Why can we say that it was primarily an act of grace?

2. Try to think of common, everyday "signs" that serve as reminders of relationships, like wedding rings and road signs. What is similar and different about the rainbow as a sign?

3. Discuss the importance of the Flood in terms of God's historically unfolding design to save the world.

4. Many ancient civilizations had traditions of a great flood. How can we account for this? Why should we accept the Bible's account as the one true record?

5. What was so evil about the Tower of Babel movement? Are there any modern parallels to this ancient effort?

## For Further Study:

Bright, J., "Has Archaeology Found Evidence for the Flood?," in *The Biblical Archaeology Reader*, (Garden City, N.J., Doubleday, Anchor Books, 1961).

De Graaf, S.G., *Promise and Deliverance*, (St. Catherines, Ont., Paideia Press, 1977) I, pp. 59-74.

Unger, M.F., *Archaeology and the Bible* (Grand Rapids, Zondervan, 1956).

Vos, G., *Biblical Theology*, (Grand Rapids, Eerdmans, 1948) Part I, Chapters 5 & 6.

Wooley, C.L., *Ur of the Chaldees*, (New York, W. W. Norton, 1965).

# Abrahamic Epoch of Biblical Revelation

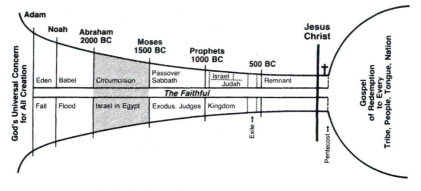

I. The Call of Abraham.

    A. Divine Initiative.

    B. Separated to God's Service.

    C. The Promise of a Son.

II. Running Ahead of God's Plan.

III. An Agreement Between Friends.

    A. Parties to the Covenant.

    B. Obligations of the Covenant.

    C. Confirming Sign of the Covenant.

IV. Circumcision: Sacrament of Belonging.

V. A Promised Son is Born.

VI. Historical Summary.

Scripture Readings
    Genesis 12-50
    Matthew 1:1-17
    John 8
    Romans 4-9
    Galatians 3:6-25

## CHAPTER FIVE

# *Abrahamic Epoch of Biblical Revelation*

ABRAHAM stands as a towering figure in Bible history. In God's relation to Abraham we see the saving purposes for the world more clearly. For the first time there is a Sacrament, Circumcision, to serve as a reminder of a special Divine/human relationship. The promises made to Abraham are repeatedly identified as "everlasting" which emphasizes their enduring nature. No wonder then that both Old and New Testaments have scores of references to Abraham, especially in the context of assurances that the God of Abraham is a promise-keeping God. Abraham is mentioned by name 234 times in the Old Testament. That should not surprise us. Additionally, the New Testament contains 62 references to Abraham. That is a remarkable fact to which our attention must be drawn. Notably, the Song of Mary anticipates the birth of Jesus as evidence of God's faithfulness "remembering to be merciful to Abraham and his descendants forever, even as He said to our fathers." (Luke 2:54 & 55) The apostle Paul identifies believers in Christ as children of Abraham. "If you belong to Christ, then you are Abraham's seed, and heirs according to the promise" (Galatians 3:29). Clearly, Abraham, and the revelation given through him is crucially important in salvation history.

Abraham was the first Hebrew. He is so called in Genesis 14:13. While the origin of the name is not certain, the discovery of the Mari Letters dating back to the eighteenth century B.C. may clarify its source for us. The term "habiru" appears frequently in these letters, the fundamental meaning of which seems to be "a wanderer" or "one who crosses over" or "one who passes from one place to another." Such a designation fits Abraham and the early patriarchs well. Since consonants are more enduring in language development than vowels, the movement from "habiru" to "hebrew" is quite expected across linguistic lines. Furthermore, the city of Mari was located on the middle Euphrates, midway between Ur to the south and Haran in the north. When Abraham, Terah, and Lot with their families and herds left Ur in southern Mesopotamia, they must have traveled through Mari. It was a thriving city and commercial center at that time, and the only place for many miles where a caravan could be resupplied. To the local populous Abraham's people were indeed wanderers. They had no abiding city but found their security in obeying God's call and going wherever that led them. They were Hebrews, passing from one place to another as God led them. God risked His reputation with them as His chosen ones through whom the blessing of salvation for the whole world would eventually come.

## The Call of Abraham

God called Abraham out of an environment of false religions to a life in which God would stand in the center. Through Abraham all nations of the earth would eventually participate in the genuinely fulfilling God-centered life. Genesis 12 opens with this divine call:

> The Lord said to Abram, Leave your country, your people, and your father's household and go to the land I will show you. I will make you into a great nation and I will bless you; I will make your name great and you will be a blessing.

> I will bless those who bless you, and whoever curses you, I will curse; and all peoples on earth will be blessed through you. (Genesis 12:1-3)

Even Abraham could not have imagined the world and history embracing extent of the consequences of this call. Indeed, 2000 years of Bible history would have to unfold before the possibility of the fulfillment of this promise could become reality.

The call of Abraham is by divine initiative. Always in Biblical revelation God does the choosing and the human side of the relationship must obediently respond. God's choice of Abraham as a covenant partner in the plan of salvation is an election for service. Johannes Blauw makes this point emphatically in his book entitled *The Missionary Nature of the Church*. "The purpose of the election is service, and when the service is withheld, the election loses its meaning, and therefore fails" (p. 22). The "election for service" emphasis is strongly emphasized in Genesis 18:19,

> For I have chosen him, so that he will direct his children and his household after him to keep the way of the Lord by doing what is right and just, so that the Lord will bring about for Abraham what he has promised him.

God's choice of Abraham as a covenant partner did not make him the Lord's pampered favorite to be coddled and lavished with gifts and provided a soft life free from threats and concerns. To be the Lord's faithful servant implies responsibility in the context of an active life. So Abraham has to uproot himself and move to a new country (Gen. 12:4-9), face the threat of famine and move again (Gen. 12:10) and is tempted to hide behind a half-truth (Sarah was his half-sister as well as his wife) when he felt endangered (Gen. 12:11-20).

One of the factors indicating the authentic realism of the Bible in contrast to other "scriptures" is the humanness of the personalities recorded. They are real people, not romanticized, idealized figures, of which the mythology of other traditions is full. Here we have Abraham, that lofty personality in Bible history, giving evidence of human weakness. God chose a real human being with recognizable imperfections as His covenant partner, to fulfill His redemptive work. This is, of course, also true of all human agents in salvation history.

The real-life quality of Abraham's experiences is also demonstrated in chapters thirteen and fourteen of Genesis. They record the realization of fellowship with God in the context of life's trials, joys, conflicts, and challenges. Worship of God is interspersed with common duties and responsibilities. Abraham built altars for the worship of the Lord (13:4 & 13:18) in the flow of a busy life of administrating his possessions (13:5 & 6) and resolving conflicts between his employees and those of his nephew Lot. Genesis fourteen adds the matter of political relationships (14:1-12), military ventures (14:13-16) and stewardship responsibilities (14:17-24) which needed attention. All of this emphasizes that Abraham was a very real, human, historical personality because of whose partnership with God "all peoples on earth will be blessed."

The essence of Abraham's call was to be separated unto the Lord's service. He and his descendants after him were always to recognize themselves as a separate people. They would live among the nations but not be part of them; in the world but not of the world. Whenever Abraham, and especially his descendants, failed it was invariably at this point. They tried to imitate the life and religion of the non-separated, unwilling to be different from those not called to the Lord's service. We shall observe examples of such failings both in Abraham's experience and that of his descendants recorded later in Scripture. The faithfulness of the Lord, who fulfills His purposes through humanly flawed means, will stand out in bolder relief by comparison.

Perhaps the most remarkable statement about Abraham in the Bible is found outside the Genesis account. James 2:23 reads, "Abraham believed God, and it was credited to him as righteousness, and he was called God's friend." Two other references to Abraham as the friend of God are found in II Chronicles 20:7 and Isaiah 41:8. This friendship with the Almighty came at the price of separation from the God-dishonoring aspects of worldly existence. As James also observes in chapter 4 verse 11, "Don't you know that friendship with the world is hatred toward God? Anyone who chooses to be a friend of the world is an enemy of God."

The intimacy of this divine/human friendship is demonstrated by the manner in which God took Abraham into His confidence. "Shall I hide from Abraham what I am about to do?" (Genesis 18:17). What God intended to do through the call of Abraham His friend was to extend this friendship to all of Abraham's spiritual seed. Those who would come to faith in Abraham's God would also come to know friendship with the Almighty. The transformation of human beings from enmity and hostility toward God to renewed friendship was the ultimate purpose for which Abraham was called in his own time. The coming of Christ would eventually assure the result. As Jesus said two thousand years later to His disciples and through them to us, "I have called you friends, for everything that I have learned from my Father I have made known to you" (John 15:15). Abraham is the original type of those from all nations who, through faith in Christ, would become friends of God.

The primary and immediate need for the realization of God's promises to Abraham was a son. How could all nations be eventually blessed through his offspring if there were none? The concern expressed in Genesis 15:2 is easy to understand. "O Sovereign Lord, what can you give me since I remain childless?" According to the social custom of the time, the senior member from among a master's servants would inherit the estate if there were no physical progeny. But Abraham was assured that his own flesh and blood son would serve as the agency through whom the promises of God would be accomplished. Following this reassuring revelation we have Abraham's believing response (Gen. 15:6). At eighty-five years of age it took a large measure of faith, especially in view of the dimensions of the promise. Offspring as impossible to number as the stars above and the sands of the earth!

The promises God gave to Abraham included the land of Canaan as his possession in addition to the legacy of unnumbered people (Genesis 15:7). As confirmation of the eventual inheritance of the land by his descendants, a ceremonial sacrifice was engaged (Genesis 15:8-19). Confirmation of covenant agreements by sacrifice was a key element in formal relationships in the patriarchal era. So here we have a blood-letting ceremony as a solemn assurance to Abraham that Canaan will stand as an everlasting possession for descendants without number (Genesis 15:5 & 18; 17:8). The manner in which Christ makes possible the fulfillment of this promise of Caanan as an everlasting possession will be clarified in chapter eight.

### Running Ahead of God's Plan

We cannot be certain of the number of years that passed between the confirmation of the covenant promises in Genesis fifteen and the events recorded in chapter sixteen. We do know that Abraham was eighty-six and Sarah seventy-six years old when the promise of a son was first given. Their impatience to have a child who would be the first of populous generations to follow is not difficult to understand considering their advanced years. The attempt to provide a human solution for the fulfillment of the divine promise was tempting. It also reflected a lack of faith and ended in disaster.

Sarah's suggestion that Abraham have a child through a relationship with the servant girl Hagar was in keeping with the social customs of the time. The Nuzu Tablets, dating back to the fifteenth century, constitute a unique commentary on the period near the close of the Abrahamic Epoch. They record marriage customs that provided for a barren wife to select one of her slave girls as her substitute to bear a child with her husband. It is interesting to note that the wife was required to take the initiative in this matter just as Sarah does. (Genesis 16:1 & 2)

While this practice followed perfectly acceptable social custom of the time, Abraham and Sarah may not be excused for following it. They were called to separate themselves unto the Lord's service and from the pagan religious and social patterns of their environment. Recourse to human practices can never serve to justify one's behavior before the Lord. Clearly Abraham's approving response to Sarah's initiative had him running ahead of the Lord's will and ended disappointingly. Hostility between the women in Abraham's household was the result, a conflict which continues among Abraham's descendants to the present, as daily reports from the Middle East confirm. Arabs and Israeli alike trace their origin to Abraham and many Arabs relate to Abraham directly through the Ishmael line. Hagar herself was an Egyptian.

Sarah's treatment of Hagar and her son is inexcusable. It is true that Hagar's arrogance precipitated Sarah's reaction, but more humane and responsible behavior should be expected from one who is called to be the mother of nations. She was a participant in the fulfillment of divine promise, one from whom more noble behavior should have been expected. Even on the basis of accepted social custom of the times Sarah's actions cannot be justified. Her ethical standards didn't even measure up to the prevailing customs. The Nuzu Tablets illuminate the responsibility of the mistress to take her slave girl's child as her own. It was further provided that a son born to a slave wife could never be expelled and disinherited. Impatient human intervention was detrimental within the situation in which God's promises were to be progressively unfolded. Patient submission to the divine agenda was necessary before promise could become reality.

### An Agreement Between Friends (Genesis 17)

God called Abraham into a special relationship many years prior to the formal establishment of the covenant. It wasn't until the ninety-ninth year of his life that Abraham was introduced to the nature of his relationship to God in a very specific and detailed way. Genesis chapter seventeen lays out the promises and obligations of the covenant partners. We shall analyze the nature of this relationship in terms of the basic three essential elements of all covenants. These include (1) the parties to the covenant, (2) the stipulations and obligations each assumes, and (3) the confirming sign (signature) of participation in the agreement.

The parties to the covenant are God as party of the first part and Abraham, with his descendants, as party of the second part. God as first party and Initiator is emphasized in the words, "I am God Almighty;" "I will confirm my covenant;" "I will make you very fruitful;" "I will give as an everlasting possession;" etc. Clearly, this is not a relationship of equals but of a Superior who takes the lead and calls subordinates into intimate union of purpose with Himself. Abraham as representative second party is addressed in the second person. "(You) walk before me and be blameless;" "You will be the father of many nations;" "You must keep my covenant, you and your descendants after you;" etc (Genesis 17:1-8).

Each side of the arrangement assumes very specific obligations for the continuation of the relationship. From the divine side comes the responsibility to be Abraham's God and the God of his descendants. This promise includes the full range of meaning that, Biblically, attaches to "God." A God of salvation, grace, love, and providence on behalf of parties to His covenant. Further, God obligates Himself to multiply Abraham's offspring, to provide a land of promise, and to preserve covenant forever. The human side is obligated to a life of obedience and holiness ("walk before me and be blameless"), to live patiently awaiting fulfillment of promise, and to practice circumcision as a confirming sign of the relationship established.

All contractual agreements require official confirmation signs before they are considered to be in force. Marriages require a license signed by the parties to the covenant. Building contractors have documents formulated which identify the participants, indicate the blueprinted specifications, and require signatures of both contractor and purchaser. So it is that God's dealings with human beings in the history of redemption took the form of a relationship requiring confirmation through official signs. We observed in regard to the Noahic Epoch that the rainbow was identified as a sign. "I have set my rainbow in the clouds, and it will be the sign of the covenant between me and the whole earth." (Genesis 9:13) In the Garden of Eden, the tree of life, designated as a test of obedience, served as a sign of the divine/human relationship. We may define a sign as *a continuing reminder, to both parties, of the obligations and privileges of their relationship.*

At the great juncture of Bible history when Abraham represents the human side of the covenant, another sign is introduced. This is not a new covenant, but a new stage in the continuing relationship throughout redemptive history between God and humanity. The one plan of redemption moves deliberately according to the divine plan through clearly defined epochs. In the process, the divine intentions become increasingly clear and specific, even in regard to the signs established. Circumcision, the sign introduced at this point, is the first *sacramental* sign in the Bible record. It is important to distinguish between "general signs" such as the rainbow, and "sacramental signs" such as circumcision.

A *general* sign is simply "there" to be observed as a reminder of a recognized relationship with God. Thus the rainbow, whenever observed by God and human beings, is a reminder of the assured promise that a catastrophic flood on the dimensions of the original one will never again occur. As a phenomenon of nature, the rainbow is a broadly universal sign. A *sacramental* sign is also a reminder of a relationship with the Lord. But it is much more than a passive reminder, and has a narrowly restricted application. For one thing, a sacramental sign is a repeatable rite or practice that can be deliberately celebrated on specific occasions. In addition, and very significantly, a sacrament carries a message of salvation through shed blood and, therefore, has its fullest meaning in its reference to redemption through Jesus Christ and His cross. And, finally, a sacramental sign identifies celebrants as members of a believing community of faith. Those who celebrate a sacrament engage in a conscious act of faith which marks them as members of a fellowship of believers. It is a distinguishing, dividing act, not intended for unrestricted, general application, but provided as an identification mark for a restricted community of the faithful.

The establishment of a sacramental sign as a mark of identity for those within the believing community points up the enormous importance of the revelation at this point in salvation history. What was established with Abraham carries through consistently in all the rest of the Bible. To understand the Divine/human relationship as outlined with Abraham and his extended household goes far to understand all that follows.

## Circumcision: Sacrament of Belonging

Circumcision was the sacrament of identification for those whose privilege and responsibility it was to be members of the God-fearing community. Those within the fellowship were circumcised, those outside were the uncircumcised. Those within were no better than those outside. To think and act as though they were was unwarranted pride and impugned the grace and mercy of God whose providence placed them in their privileged position. Their privilege consisted in the fact of membership in a fellowship where God was honored, where His will was the standard for faith and life, where the promise of an eventual Seed of a woman to destroy the kingdom of evil was the hope by which they lived, and where each could treat the other with dignity as an object of God's gracious choice. In short, circumcision was an external mark identifying those who enjoyed a special relationship with God. The practice itself did not put anyone into such a relationship but was an acknowledgment that God had called them to be His possession. It was a recognition of an objective situation.

With privilege came responsibility. Those called into fellowship with God were set apart for His service. This required lives of faithful obedience to their God. They were especially commanded to teach succeeding generations the past mighty acts of God and the promise of great future events through which all nations would come to know the salvation of the Lord. The continuity of the believing community depended on the faithfulness of each generation. Each assumed responsibility for instructing the next.

The pattern for the administration of circumcision during two thousand years of Old Testament history was established with Abraham. It involved a minor surgical procedure for the removal of a small portion of the protective covering of the tip of the male reproductive organ. The involvement of the male organ should not be overlooked in its importance. It stands as a vivid reminder that succeeding generations unborn, and yet genetically potential, would share in the relationship with God and His promises that the ceremony implies.

The administration of circumcision was intended for natural born sons of believing parents, adopted sons of believers, adult males who became believers and their infant sons. Ishmael, circumcised at age thirteen is an example of a natural son of Abraham. Eliezar, born in Damascus but adopted by Abraham, was circumcised as were all the servants in his household with their male children. These servants are described as "bought from a foreigner" (Genesis 17:27) which was the method by which people were adopted at that time. Since these adopted family members also belonged to the community of faith in which God was honored and His will obeyed, they too were part of the privileged fellowship and received the mark of participation in it. Then, finally, infant sons one week after birth were circumcised of which Isaac was the first example (Genesis 24:4). There was, therefore, provision both for what may be called infant circumcision and believer's circumcision.

The relationship for which circumcision stood as the external confirming sign was emphatically spiritual and not biological. From the outset, the majority of those in Abraham's household who were circumcised were not his physical descendants. They were, with their children, purchased servants and therefore adopted out of pagan religious environments. Their assimilation into a believing household qualified them to receive the mark of identity as God's privileged people. Subsequent history reinforces the importance of spiritual faith rather than physical relatedness. Ishmael, a physical descendant of Abraham, grew up to reject the promises and responsibilities of covenant with God and therefore denied the meaning of his circumcision. Eliezar, of pagan parentage, is a prime example of one who was faithful to the obligations and special relationship with Abraham's God for which circumcision was the external confirming sign (Genesis 24:27).

There are frequent examples in the Bible of those who substituted a physical relationship with Abraham as of first importance. If they could trace their genealogy back to father Abraham they thought they could live as they pleased and still be accepted in the fellowship of God's people. They proudly identified themselves as "the circumcised" and trusted in the external form to make them right with God. Jesus had to warn people of His time that physical descendancy did not guarantee acceptance with Abraham's God (John 8:39-41). What was required was a heartfelt devotion to the Lord, a living faith in the God of their salvation, not a barren formal relationship that trusted in outward forms.

The contrast between a vital versus a formal relationship in covenant with God is one that runs consistently through the Bible record. The majority appear to be content with formal membership

in established religion. More often than not the religious professionals were among those content with a routine formalism. It was
left to a faithful minority to recognize that only a vital relationship
of faith could make the outward forms precious and meaningful.
The true descendants of Abraham were not those who went through
the formality of the circumcision rite but those who understood that
the external rite was a call to a living faith in the God who set them
apart for His service. The Apostle Paul says it so clearly in address-
ing New Testament believers. "Understand then that those who
believe are children of Abraham," and "those who have faith are
blessed along with Abraham who had faith." (Galatians 3:7 and 9;
cf. Romans 9:8)

Circumcision was intended for males only. They served as
representative of the whole believing community. It is the only
sacrament in the Bible which was restricted to one sex. At this point
in the history of revelation this restriction was not surprising. The
Old Testament was a time which may be called *representational.*
Direct access to God was severely limited to designated representatives. All others had to have intermediaries or be represented by
those designated to do so. Human mediators stood as types of the
Perfect Mediator who was to come to stand between human beings
and God in perfection. Adam, Noah, and Abraham served in this
typical capacity. Later Moses and Joshua would. Then a long line
of levitical priests would serve as representative mediators. Even
the sacrificial lambs on the worship altars represented the repentant
sinner who deserved the fate of his sacrificial representative. And in
circumcision boys and men represented the entire believing community which included girls and women. Not till Christ, the sinners
perfect representative priest and sacrificial lamb, does the
representative model cease. He became the only mediator through
whom we all have access to the Heavenly Father. After His coming
the representational time is over and all have access to the forms and
privileges of the community of faith.

### A Promised Son is Born

The promise of a son was given initially to Abraham when he was
eighty-five years old (Genesis 15:1-6). It was repeated when he
was ninety-nine (Genesis 17:15-22). In response to the first
revelation we read that "Abram believed the Lord, and he credited
to him as righteousness." It took a large measure of faith, at his age,

to believe that a son of promise would be born. Sarah's age of about seventy-five years may have made the test of faith even greater.

Fourteen years had passed and Sarah still showed no signs of impending motherhood when the promise was repeated. This time Abraham could not believe it. He laughed the cynical laughter of unbelief. Under his breath he said to himself, "Ninety-nine year old men and eighty-nine year old women do not have babies." (Genesis 17:17) Then he offered the Lord a humanly reasonable solution. "If only Ishmael might live under your blessing." (Genesis 17:18) Ishmael was a strapping young thirteen-year-old at the time. For him to be the one through whom a promised people could result was humanly possible and believable. Why should God risk His reputation by promising too much, promising the impossible? The Lord's response was to insist that Sarah would indeed have a son within a year. His name must be Isaac, which means "he laughs," as a continuing reminder that when God makes a promise, don't laugh in unbelief.

Isaac was born, a promised son as an important link in the golden chain which culminated in *the* Promised Son of Abraham, the Lord Jesus Christ. Through *that* Son, Abraham has surely been a blessing to all nations. As Jesus said, "Abraham rejoiced at the thought of seeing my day; he saw it and was glad." (John 8:56)

### Historical Summary--Abrahamic Epoch

During the Biblical time period from Abraham (2000 B.C.) to Moses (1500 B.C.) those descendants who remained faithful to God continued to live by the truth of the revelation as given to Abraham. That is to say they affirmed their faith in Abraham's God, centered their worship life around altar sacrifices of animals, and circumcised all male descendants and converts from paganism as a mark of God's ownership upon them and His special relation to them. They also trusted the Lord to fulfill the promises of a geographical homeland as well as offspring as numberless as the stars.

Of the eight known sons of Abraham which Hagar, Sarah, and Keturah bore (Genesis 25:1-4), only Isaac was faithful to the revelation given to his father. And of all Abraham's grandsons of which there must have been scores, only one, Jacob, was a faithful believer. Thus, just two generations after Abraham, the revelational agents, God's special people, were narrowed to a single patriarchal house, Jacob's. His descendants, therefore, became crucially important in the history of God's saving concern for the world.

Since Jacob's name was changed later in life to Israel (Genesis 32:28), his descendants were called Israelites. From his time onward, the Old Testament concerns itself with the history of Israel, the chosen people through whom God promised to provide a Savior for the world. Genesis 28-50 records the rise and growth of the Nation of Israel during a period lasting 450 years. Most of that time was spent in Egypt, first as a privileged minority for a brief time and then as a severely oppressed minority. Were it not for divine intervention, this people, upon whom so much depended for all the world and for all time to come, would have been annihilated. But God did intervene, mightily, opening a new and dramatic chapter in salvation history with Moses and a delivered people.

**Discussion Stimulators, Chapter Five**

1. Enumerate several factors which serve to emphasize the prominent place Abraham occupies in Bible history.

2. The purpose of God's call to Abraham and his faithful descendants was that they should be a "separate" people. From what and for what were they to be separated?

3. What are the three basic elements of all contractual agreements or covenants? Observe how contracts or covenants formalize and structure most relationships in human society.

4. Distinguish between a "general sign" as a reminder of the God/humanity relationship and a "sacramental" sign.

5. Circumcision was a sacrament identifying those whose privilege and responsibility it was to be included in a community of God's people. What were some of those privileges and responsibilities?

6. The relationship for which circumcision stood as the confirming sign was primarily spiritual rather than biological. Explain.?

**For Further Study:**

Blauw, J. *The Missionary Nature of the Church,* (London, Lutterworth Press, 1962).

Boyd, Robert T., *Tells, Tombs, and Treasurers,* (New York, Bonanza Books, 1969) Pages 80-106.

De Graaf, S.G., *Promise and Deliverance,* (St. Catherines, Ont., Paideia Press, 1977) I, pp. 75-252.

Jessop, H. E., *Abraham the Hebrew,* (Kansas City, Beacon Hill Press, 1958).

Thompson, J. A., *The Bible and Archaeology,* (Grand Rapids, Eerdmans, 1972) Chapter 2.

Unger, Merrill F., *Famous Archaeological Discoveries,* (Grand Rapids, Zondervan, 1965) Chapters 6 and 8.

Vos, Gerhardus, Biblical Theology, (Grand Rapids, Eerdmans, 1948) Part 1, Chapter 7.

# Mosaic Epoch of Biblical Revelation

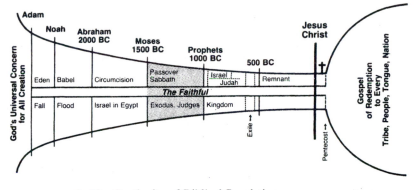

I. The Continuity of Biblical Revelation.

II. The Exodus: Deliverance for God's Service.

    A. From Political Bondage.

    B. From Religious Enslavement.

III. Divine Power and Grace Displayed.

IV. The Passover: Sacrament of Deliverance.

V. The Law of Life for God's People.

    A. The Response of Gratitude.

    B. The Motive of Love.

VI. The Sabbath: Reflecting the Divine Pattern.

VII. Historical Summary: Mosaic Epoch

Scripture Readings
    Exodus
    Deuteronomy
    Joshua
    Judges
    Psalm 105
    Psalm 106 Psalm 135
    Psalm 136

# Mosaic Epoch
# of Biblical Revelation

MIDWAY between Abraham and David in Biblical history stands Moses. Under him the nation of Israel comes into its own as the carrier of redemption. God's saving concern for the world is demonstrated in the preservation of Israel as a people, their deliverance from Egyptian oppression, and their eventual settling in the Promised Land. The proximate purpose for God's revelatory engagement with Israel was to demonstrate His power and grace before all the nations. Against all odds Israel survived only because of the Lord's promise, "I will redeem you with an outstretched arm and with great acts of judgment." (Exodus 6:6) The ultimate purpose for God's gracious partnership with Israel was to continue through them the plan of redemption promised to their forefathers which was finally realized when the Savior of the world arrived on the human scene.

## The Continuity of Biblical Revelation

The emphasis throughout the Bible's account of revelation at the time of Moses is upon the continuity with truth revealed earlier. This juncture in Biblical history is not a new dispensation abruptly introduced in contrast with that which precedes and follows it. Rather there is an organic relation between the truth revealed in the various epochs. The truth progressively unfolds, like a growing plant from seed, through the developing organism, to the flower and fruit stage. The seed of promise was given already with Adam and Eve. The seed germinated and sprouted a promising stem with Noah, the beginnings of branches with Abraham, developing clusters of leaves with Moses, the appearance of buds during the long Prophetic Epoch, culminating in the flower of perfection which is the Lord Jesus Christ. One could add that the fruit of the whole process is the New Testament Church, the Body of Christ, the temple of the Holy Spirit.

This emphasis upon the continuity of revelation is not mechanically imposed out of interpretive eagerness to establish relation between various Biblical periods. The record of the revelation itself during the Mosaic time frame acknowledges the continuity with that which preceded. According to Exodus 2:24 it was because of God's faithfulness to His commitment to Abraham that Israel could be confident that their plea for deliverance would be heard by the Lord. Five hundred years of history had passed, but their ever-faithful God "remembered His covenant with Abraham, with Isaac, and with Jacob." God's great intervention on behalf of Israel was rooted in His unchangeable promises made earlier. This is confirmed clearly in Exodus 6:6-8:

> Therefore, say to the Israelites: I am the Lord and I will bring you out from under the yoke of the Egyptians. I will free you from being slaves to them and I will redeem you with an outstretched arm and with mighty acts of judgment. I will take you as my own people, and I will be your God. And I will bring you to the land I swore with uplifted hand to give to Abraham, to Isaac and to Jacob.

To understand the truth revealed during the Mosaic Epoch requires that we view it as "in addition to" rather than "in place of" prior revelation. Truth builds upon truth till the climax is reached in Him who is THE truth and the life.

## The Exodus: Deliverance for God's Service

Israel's deliverance from Egyptian oppression partakes of a two-fold character. They were rescued both from political bondage and from religious paganism. Of the two, the deliverance from false gods and false worship styles was the more significant. One could say that their release from political servitude was necessary so that they could escape from a pagan environment. So long as they were politically enslaved they could not be free to serve the purpose for which God had chosen them as His people. The message Moses was charged to bring to Pharaoh emphasized this point. "This is what the Lord says: Israel is my firstborn son. Let my son go that he may worship me" (Exodus 4:22 & 23). Enslavement to a pagan power prevented them from the service that commitment to the true God required.

To understand the role which the plagues filled in God's acts of deliverance of His people we must be aware of the religious conflict implied. The plagues were not simply the cause of great suffering designed to break down Egyptian resistance to Moses' demands to "let my people go." They were, primarily, demonstrations of the superiority of Jahweh over the pagan gods of the land. "I will bring judgment on all the gods of Egypt. I am the Lord" (Exodus 12:12). The religion of Egypt was an idolatry which deified the forces of nature. Nature's vegetation was recognized as the source of food to sustain life and therefore identified with the divine in reality. Since water is absolutely essential to nourish both plants and humans, the Nile was especially venerated. It was viewed as the divine sustainer of life in a climate where it virtually never rains. Even cattle, especially cows and oxen, came in for worshipful regard since they represented so well the reproductive forces of nature. They provided the milk to make babies grow and fertilizer for abundant vegetation. The "sacred cow" religious syndrome has always been an indicator of the worship of some "power" within the created order instead of the Creator Himself. Hinduism is a modern example.

The plagues exposed the powerlessness of naturalistic deities before the God of heaven (Exodus 7-11). The waters of the Nile were turned blood red. Frogs, gnats, and flies infested the natural environment. Livestock and humans became diseased. Hail and locusts spread destruction before which nature gods were helpless. The sun, the life-giving "god" of the heavens, was darkened for three days. And, finally, the first-born fruit of human fertility was destroyed. Since Pharaoh refused to allow Jahweh's first born spiritual son to depart, Pharaoh and his people lost their first-born physical sons.

The majority within the nation of Israel never seemed to keep their true destiny in focus. Under Moses they repeatedly failed to understand the religious purpose of their calling. They assumed that Jahweh was a private national deity who would treat them like His pampered favorites regardless of their unfaithlessness. Within months after the Lord brought them safely out of Egypt they reverted to religious practices they had learned in pagan Egypt. The golden calf was a fertility god representation directly related to the sacred cows and bulls of their former religious environment. To this calf they sacrificed and credited it with delivering them from Egypt (Exodus 32:8). They may even have indulged in the sexual immorality associated with fertility cultism. (Exodus 32:6) Thus their departure from Egypt was understood in the narrowest of terms as release from political bondage to live as they pleased. If they weren't pleased with their immediate circumstances they felt justified in complaining to Moses about their condition. They even complained to the point of wishing they were back in Egypt (Exodus 16:1-3). Because of their shortsighted and selfish perspective they failed to see themselves as actors chosen by God in the great drama which led to the Promised Land and eventually to the Promised Seed. Fortunately, a faithful few had their vision clearly focused upon the fulfillment of God's will in their endeavors.

### Divine Power and Grace Displayed

While it was to the great advantage of Israel to be delivered from political and economic oppression, the primary purpose involved was the display of the power and grace of God. All the details of the account emphasize the divine strength for bringing it about. Jahweh's might is displayed in the accumulation of miracles, in the judgment of the plagues, in the dividing of waters, in the destruction of Pharaoh and his army, and in the preservation of Israel in the wilderness. Even the stubbornness of Pharaoh serves to prolong the process of deliverance to allow for the fullest display of divine omnipotence. The task was made more difficult so that the power displayed might be more apparent. In Exodus 9:16 Jahweh declares, "But I have raised you up for this very purpose that I might show you my power and that my name might be declared in all the earth." Sacred Scripture of later times repeatedly celebrated the Exodus as the mighty act of God which served as the basis for an assured hope of future deliverances.

In addition to the display of Divine power, the deliverance from Egypt was a convincing demonstration of the sovereign grace of God. It is repeatedly stated in the Pentateuch that the source of Israel's privileged relationship with Jahweh lies exclusively in divine grace. God chose them out of unmerited love, not because of any qualities possessed by the people themselves. (cf. Deut. 7:7; 9:4-6)

The Israelites were rescued and spared in spite of their association with their oppressors in idolatrous practices. True, God's choice of Mosaic Israel was traced back to his promises to the forefathers. But this carried the initiative of divine choice to a previous relationship that was itself rooted in the sovereign love of God. His gracious intervention on behalf of Israel in Egypt was a consequence of his steadfast love to the Fathers.

The idea of sonship in reference to Israel reinforced the grace of God calling her into covenant with Himself. "Israel is my firstborn son" (Exodus 4:22). Sonship is by its very nature unmerited. Whether natural born or adopted, a son is received into a relationship with parents apart from any choice on his part. Israel was constituted a corporate "son of God" in its deliverance from Egypt. The Exodus is identified in later Biblical writings as the great event in which God brought them into being as His people in order that, through them, He might reveal His gracious purpose. "When Israel was a child I loved him and called My son out of Egypt" (Hosea 11:1).

Even the nature of the term for "love" used in reference to Israel emphasizes the grace of God as foundation for her salvation. For the term implies an unmerited favor which seeks the welfare of its object. It is not a love stimulated by a recognition of something attractive or desirable in the one loved. Rather it is a disposition of gracious affection for an undeserving object. While such love desires a response of deep affection in return, it continues to love even when it is not requited. In short, it is steadfast, enduring love that never fails because it is rooted in grace.

### The Passover: Sacrament of Deliverance

The night of the execution of the last plague, when the eldest child in every Egyptian family died, was also the night in which the sacrament of the Passover was established (Exodus 12). The contrast is worth noting; destruction for those who attempt to resist the progress of God's plan of salvation in history, but deliverance for those chosen to participate in the fulfillment of that plan. The apparent severity of the judgment reflected in the tenth plague must be viewed in that light. The salvation of the world hinged on the preservation of a people through whom that salvation would be eventually realized. Opposition to the divine purpose for the world had to be effectively resisted so that future unnumbered millions could know the salvation of the Lord.

Celebrating the Passover required the sacrifice of a lamb. The grace of God was the basis for Israel's deliverance, but grace could not be exercised without atonement. Redemption through the shed blood of an innocent substitute is clearly portrayed. The application of the blood of the sacrificed victim upon the door frames of the houses placed those "under the blood" for whom expiation or payment for sin had been made. The element of purification, closely connected with that of expiation, is symbolized by the required use of hyssop to splash the blood upon the desired places. Hyssop figures everywhere in the Bible as an instrument of purification. A small, bushy plant, its stems and leaves were suitable for ceremonial sprinkling. Thus the account of the blood placed upon houses was not simply a mark of identification by which the dwellings of the Hebrews could be recognized. It assured that sacrifice had been made and purification applied for those within. People chosen for God's service must have both.

Passover required partaking of a sacrificial meal. It was a communal sacrament or a celebration of communion with fellow believers in the Lord's presence. Like circumcision, it was a sacramental sign of identification with a community of faith and served as a testimony that God is the Redeemer of His people. Unlike circumcision, it was intended for repeated celebration at regular intervals. Thus the Lord provided for an individual, once-in-a-lifetime sacrament of inclusion in the covenant community by way of circumcision. He also provided a communal sacrament so that at regular intervals the household of faith could celebrate and reaffirm their relationship as the redeemed people of the Lord. Parallels in this regard with the form of the sacraments of Baptism (one-time individual sacrament) and Holy Communion (repeated communal sacrament) in the Apostolic Epoch of New Testament times will be clarified in Chapter Eight.

Passover was established as a sacrament by which all future generations would celebrate the mighty act of God's deliverance of His people from bondage. The sacramental character of the commemorative meal focused attention upon the religious nature of Israel's deliverance. If attention is focused primarily upon the political and economic enslavement of the people of Israel the essential issue of deliverance from false religion is missed. In order for a people of God to spring into existence for effective service as carriers of hope and salvation they must be cut loose from a world opposed to God. Egyptian power in this respect is typical of the forces of evil which prevent the true worship of God and witness of His grace in the world. The condition of Israel in Egypt was one of political oppression and harsh bondage. They were slaves. It may have been the hope of liberation from political enslavement that was uppermost in the minds of the majority. Yet the emphasis needs to be placed upon liberation for God's service, rather than liberation from oppression as an end in itself. If there is a liberation theology inherent here it must be understood in terms of the freedom necessary to live as fulfillers of a divine calling in the world, not simply as a redress of political grievances and social injustice as ends in themselves.

## The Law of Life for God's People

Israel as a nation was intended to be a Theocracy. That is, the rule of God was to be recognized as supreme over all aspects of personal and national life. Accordingly, God's will was the required standard for determining moral duty in all relationships, not social custom or humanly imposed practices. It was in the Decalogue, or Ten Commandments that the responsibility before God was most clearly defined (Exodus 20). All moral injunctions enforced within the Theocratic society were situational applications of the Decalogue (Exodus 21-31).

The introduction to the Decalogue sums up what Jahweh had done for Israel. "I am the Lord your God, who brought you out of Egypt, out of the land of slavery" (Exodus 20:2). It strikingly illustrates the redemptive perspective necessary to understand the place of the Law in the life of God's people. It is because the Lord is the redeemer of His people that obedience to the Law is required. Obeying the law was the response of gratitude expected on the part of those called into privileged fellowship with the Lord. Legalists in the Israelite tradition reversed this order. They made of the Law a code of conduct by which they could merit the status as God's people. As though human conformity to a moral code could bring them into a right relation to the Lord. Not human initiative but divine deliverance was the starting point for the Law. The gospel-element is present here, for the God of grace has intervened on behalf of His own and proceeds to reveal the shape of the life of gratitude expected from those who have experienced the salvation of their God.

The motivation for obedience to the Law was love. This is not an observation for which we have to consult the New Testament to affirm. The second reading of the Commandments (Deuteronomy 5) was followed by Moses' clear implication that obedience was the joyful responsibility in the ordinary daily routine of those who love the Lord.

> Love the Lord your God with all your heart and with all your soul and with all your strength. These commandments that I give you today are to be upon your hearts. Impress them on your children. Talk about them when you sit at home and when you walk along the road, when you lie down and when you get up (Deuteronomy 6:5-7).

The Decalogue is clearly reflected in a practical applicatory manner in Leviticus 19:1-19a. There the emphasis is upon responsibility to fellowmen and the conclusion brings together Law, God, and neighbor. "Love your neighbor as yourself. I am the Lord. Keep my decrees" (Leviticus 19:18 & 19). Jesus' summary of the Law (Matthew 22:37-40) combines the Deuteronomy and Leviticus references.

The Decalogue had its initial application within the national life of Israel. But that does not detract from the universal application of it. Gerhardus Vos observes that "we must remember that the history of Israel was shaped by God intentionally to mirror all important situations befalling the people of God in all subsequent ages" (*Biblical Theology,* p. 131). We are not surprised then to find frequent summaries of the Decalogue in the New Testament with the clear inference that loyalty to the Lord is demonstrated by obedience to His commandments by New Testament believers (cf. Romans 13:8-10; James 2:8-13). Even the introductory statement of deliverance from Egyptian bondage has wider application than Israel as a nation. When Jahweh appeals to redemption from Egypt as a motive for obedience, He appeals to that which has its spiritual analogy in the life of all believers of all time. Liberation from bondage to sinful oppression of any variety is necessary to allow for the freedom to live in willing obedience to the Lord.

In contrast to the Decalogue, or Moral Law, the Civil Laws and Ceremonial Laws partook of a provisional and, therefore, temporary character. Civil Laws regulated the public life of Israel and Ceremonial Laws ordered the cultic worship life of the nation. The

Civil Laws were designed to preserve Israel as a national entity through whom the Messiah could be revealed. They regulated the public life of the nation with rules governing property rights, payment of debts, employer/employee relations, civil penalties for law breaking and many other matters. The Ceremonial Laws regulated the religious sacrificial system which anticipated the substitutionary work of Messiah as the suffering Lamb of God who would atone for the sins of the world. Upon His arrival, the purpose of Civil and Ceremonial injunctions was fulfilled. Salvation was "of the Jews" so that it could be "for the nations." Prescribed ritual forms have been set aside to make way for a universal community of believers to worship "in spirit and in truth." But the Moral Law endures as the standard of obedience by which believers express their gratitude for divine salvation. This matter will receive further clarification in Chapter Eight.

### The Sabbath: Reflecting the Divine Pattern

The special significance of the Sabbath law beginning with the Mosaic Epoch should not be overlooked. The seven-day week was certainly known before the time of Moses (cf. Genesis 29:27). But the Sabbath day in the weekly sequence takes on sacramental importance during the Mosaic Epoch time period in redemption history. The very terminology used to introduce the Sabbath requirement in Exodus 31:12-16 carries strong reminders of terms used for the sacraments of Circumcision (Genesis 17:9-14) and Passover (Exodus 12:12-14). All three are called "signs" which we have previously identified as "reminders of a relationship." Further, they are all enjoined for "the generations to come," a reference which we understand to mean "as long as human life continues." And each one is introduced as "a lasting ordinance" or "an everlasting covenant." Such terminology forces us to recognize that the relationship between God and His people celebrated by these observances is an enduring, unending relationship.

When the Bible identifies the relationship between God and His people as "everlasting" we may not understand it in an historically terminated way. We should also expect, as Biblical revelation progressively develops, that the signs will continue to be present, even if modifications in their practiced forms appear. We shall see that changes in the mode of celebration of these "signs" do indeed appear in the New Testament while the essential meaning and purpose remain. Baptism in place of Circumcision, Holy Communion in place of Passover, and the Lord's Day in place of the seventh-day Sabbath are the parallel New Testament signs of identification for those who celebrate their relationship with God. The Biblical reasons for the changes in their mode of celebration will be clarified in Chapter Eight as well as the necessity for changes in form that the New Testament revelational state of affairs required.

The principle underlying Sabbath observance is formulated in the fourth commandment. "Remember the Sabbath day by keeping it holy. For in six days the Lord made the heavens and the earth--but he rested on the seventh day" (Exodus 20:8 and 11). Believers, in their pattern of life, must copy God's creational pattern. God is the determiner of the rhythm of life for His human image bearers. With reference to God, "rest" cannot, of course, mean cessation from labor and even less a necessity for recovering from fatigue. The Old Testament usage of the word does not even require such an understanding. "Rest" in the Old Testament context has the positive suggestion of "peaceful composure." It is the state of contentment following upon diligent, productive effort. The Sabbath, therefore, stood as a thankful celebration of work successfully consummated. It provided a time for reflection with joy and satisfaction upon what was accomplished. Just as God reflected with joy and satisfaction upon His work of creation and declared it "very good" (Genesis 1:31).

It would be a mistake to base the observance of one day in seven for "rest" upon the opportunity that such a day would provide to attend to religious duties. The benefits of a weekly day of rest go beyond the cultivation of religion. For the believer, every day is a day lived in the presence of God. Daily the Lord should be honored *in* the work each one does. On the day of the Sabbath, the believer withdraws from the normal work routine to rejoice in the Lord *for* the work completed. But, while recognizing this, the reflection on God's enabling goodness, which makes productive accomplishment possible, should motivate the desire for worshipping with the assembly of believers. For worship is the richest expression of honor to the Lord. The spirit of the Sabbath reaches its highest expression, therefore, in the celebrational worship of the Lord's redeemed people. Worship and Sabbath belong together in an intimate relationship.

We have referred to the sacramental character of the Sabbath while carefully avoiding reference to the Sabbath as a sacrament. Recalling the description of the essential elements of a sacrament from Chapter Five, one element is absent in regard to the Sabbath. The absent element is the symbolic reference to salvation through shed blood. Both Circumcision and Passover included a bloody element by which the sacrifice of the Lamb of God at Calvary was anticipated. However, two other sacramental factors are present in regard to the Sabbath, namely, its "sign" character as a reminder of a relationship with God, and that it is a repeatable act of identification with a community of faith.

The lack of a specific blood-letting symbolism does not imply the lack of a redemptive typology in the Sabbath figure. On the contrary, the very structure of the week with six days for normal work routine culminating in a seventh day of rest represents the Old Testament anticipatory revelational direction. That is, the Old Testament stance was one of anticipation, looking ahead to the promise of salvation to be performed by the Messiah. The people of God had to typify in their weekly routine the future realization of redemption. As God was working through them toward the realization of redemption in Christ, so the week began with six days of work which carried them toward its culmination in a Sabbath Day of rest. The rhythmical succession of six days of labor anticipating a seventh day of joy and satisfaction was a reminder that life was moving toward a purposeful goal. It was not an aimless existence without ultimate meaning. Their purpose for existence must be focused upon their choice as God's carriers of revelation leading to the Messianic Kingdom. Even their calendar had to reflect this.

The crucial importance of the Sabbath is demonstrated repeatedly in the experience of the Israelite people. When manna was provided for food during the wilderness wanderings, it did not fall on the Sabbath (Exodus 16:26-29). Even animals and alien visitors were not to be pressed into labor on that day (Exodus 20:8-11). And foreign converts to the true faith identified their solidarity with the covenant community by, among other things, keeping the Sabbath day holy (Isaiah 56:6-7). Based upon the divine pattern in Creation, structured in relation to the redemption of Christ, the practice of observing the Sabbath always identified the Lord's people. Though modification was necessary after the coming of Christ, a

Sabbath day dimension was included in the faith life of believers after the cross also. Chapter Eight will address that issue.

### *Historical Summary--Mosaic Epoch*

For about five hundred years prior to the time of Moses believers lived by the truth revealed up to and including that revealed to Abraham. They lived in hope based upon God's promise to bless the nations through a Promised One to come. The practice of Circumcision was a sacrament of inclusion within the family of faith and exclusion from the unbelieving world. Worship life centered around altars upon which sacrificial offerings were laid in recognition of the need for forgiveness of sin and atonement or reconciliation to God.

The divine plan to redeem a lost world took on sharper and clearer light with the revelation given at the time of Moses. New initiatives in the revelation of God's will built upon all that preceded and new content was added for the faith life of those awaiting God's salvation. A listing of major contributions to the history of redemption at this point would include the following:

1. The display of God's power and grace in delivering His oppressed people from enslavement in the Exodus. They were chosen as special agents for fulfilling God's purposes in history and nothing could prevent God's determination to rescue them. This demonstration of divine power is celebrated throughout all subsequent Biblical writing.

2. The institution of the Passover as a second sacrament. It served both as a celebration of deliverance from bonadage and as an act of communal solidarity and shared faith. This sacrament was added to the sacrament of Circumcision which served to incorporate the individual within the covenant community.

3. The clearer definition of the shape which obedience to the Lord takes. Believers from Adam on knew something of the moral requirements and worship practices expected of them. But at this juncture in salvation history these expectations were made very specific and clear in the form of the Moral Law (Decalogue), Civil Law, and Ceremonial Law. A people called to be God's agents of redemption for the world must be careful to obey His rule which was a rule of love from the start, for it sought only the absolute best for those ruled.

4. The formalizing of the Sabbath requirement. The cycle of a seven day week was rooted in God's Creational activity. Under Moses the Sabbath of rest following six days of labor was formally established. As the week culminated in the reward of Sabbath rest, so the reward of a rest from evil in the salvation promised by God was anticipated.

Joshua succeeded Moses in the leadership role among the Israelites. The land of Canaan, promised about six hundred years before to Abraham, was conquered and occupied. Just before his death Joshua made a moving appeal to Israel (Joshua 24:1-27). He reminded them of the unique role they were called to play in God's plan for the world. He called them to be a faithful covenant people, a people aware of their special calling to be partners with God, agents for God's purpose. They affirmed their commitment to the Lord's service, but subsequent history demonstrated the general insincerity of their promise.

Following Joshua, three hundred twenty years of Bible history is known as the period of the Judges. The book of Judges records a very unstable time. Without any central administration, Israel was, at best, a loose confederacy of twelve tribes who cooperated only when a common defense required it. A "judge" was chosen to organize the necessary resources to resist periodic outside military threats. When the crisis was over, each tribe reverted to its independent ways. It is a testimony to divine providence that such a weak confederation would survive for over three hundred years. It reminds us that God remembers His promises even when majorities from among His human partners in covenant forget theirs.

The last of the judges, Samuel, was also a prophet who ushered in the Prophetic Epoch of Biblical history. From his time and for a thousand years thereafter the Prophets were the primary carriers of revelation. Samuel's place in Biblical history coincides with the rise of the Davidic monarchy. To this Epoch we will turn in the next chapter.

**Discussion Stimulators, Chapter Six**

1. The call to Moses to lead the people of Israel from Egyptian bondage is recorded in Exodus 3. Review this chapter to identify the clear evidences of God's initiative throughout.

2. The Exodus provided deliverance from both political oppression and from pagan religious influence. Which of these appeared to be most important to the Israelites? Are there parallels in human experience today?

3. How was the grace of God revealed and demonstrated in the event of the Exodus? How was the nature of love demonstrated?

4. Identify the similarities and differences between the two sacraments, Circumcision and Passover.

5. What was the purpose of the Law, or Ten Commandments, in the life of God's people? How was this purpose distorted? Is it possible to make a similar mistake today?

6. How was the "revelational perspective" of the Old Testament reflected in the seventh day Sabbath requirement?

7. What characteristics identified as sacramental are evident in the Sabbath requirement?

8. Identify the major contributions to the history of redemption which were revealed to us in the Mosaic Epoch.

**For Further Study:**

De Graaf, S.G., *Promise and Deliverance,* (St. Catherines, Ont., Paideia Press, 1977) I, pp. 255-418.

Halley, H.H., *Bible Handbook,* (Grand Rapids, Zondervan, 1965) pp. 109-188.

Kline, M.G., *Treaty of the Great King,* (Grand Rapids, Eerdmans, 1963).

Rosen, Ceil and Moishe, *Christ in the Passover,* (Chicago, Moody Press, 1980).

Vos, G., *Biblical Theology,* (Grand Rapids, Eerdmans, 1948) pp. 100-181.

# The Prophetic Epoch of Biblical Revelation

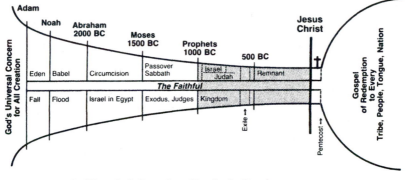

I. Historical Overview; Prophetic Epoch.

II. The Prophets: God's Guardians of the Kingdom.

    A. Obeying God as Highest Loyalty.

    B. A Costly Privilege.

III. The Message of the Prophets.

    A. Who the Lord is.

    B. Who Israel is.

    C. The Consequences of Evil.

    D. The Rewards of Righteousness.

IV. From the Exile to Christ.

    A. Exilic Prophets: Ezekial and Daniel.

    B. A Faithful Remnant Returns.

    C. Post-Exilic Prophets: Haggai and Zechariah

V. Conclusion--Prophetic Epoch.

Scripture Readings
    II Samuel
    Hosea
    Amos
    Micah
    Haggai
    Zechariah
    Ezra
    Nehemiah
    Esther

# The Prophetic Epoch
# of Biblical Revelation

THE identification of specific Epochs in Biblical history is not an arbitrary division of the process of revelation. These epochs are determined by the Biblical account itself. Whenever a momentous influx of new revelational truth is recognized in conjunction with major revelational events, a new Epoch is inaugurated. While building upon truth and influential events of past epochs, the new carries the divine saving intent for the world to a clearer and sharper level of understanding. Thus, the event of Creation and the truth revealed to Adam and Eve shaped the God/humanity relation for ages to follow. The Flood was the event and the "covenant of nature" added for the Noahic period. The call of Abraham and the promised blessings for the advantage of all nations carries revelation further into the next Epoch. The Exodus constitutes the event and the decalogue and its elaboration the revelational substance for the Mosaic Epoch. In each case a significant event accompanied by new revelation shapes the life and faith of the believing community in lasting ways for the future.

The epoch we call "Prophetic" meets the two criteria for the beginning of a new stage in the onward movement of revelation. The "event" criterion is met in the rise of the Davidic monarchy which stands as a type of the Messianic King whose expectation remains central in the hopes of the faithful thereafter. The "new revelation" requirement is met by the message and mission of the Prophets.

With the accession of David to the throne in Jerusalem, the covenant community became organized for the first time under a human ruler who was to represent the rule of Jahweh Himself.

Strictly speaking, Saul was the first king, but he was obviously not God's choice (I Samuel 8). The people wanted the wrong king for the wrong reason at the wrong time (I Samuel 8:19 & 20). Their request ran ahead of God's time-table. Almost a thousand years earlier the Lord had declared through Father Jacob that "The scepter (authority to rule) will not depart from Judah, nor the ruler's staff from between his feet until He comes to whom it belongs" (Genesis 49:10). Saul was of the tribe of Benjamin, not Judah. David's ascendancy to the throne is the objective, historical confirmation of the preeminent role the tribe of Judah filled in redemption history. A thousand years later David's Greater Son came, to whom the authority to rule really belongs. He has ascended to the Father's right hand to "rule all nations with an iron scepter" (Revelation 12:5).

This movement toward a kingdom structure of the covenant people had its rise at the time of the prophet Samuel who anointed David king. The Epoch culminated with John the Baptist who baptized Jesus and declared Him the "Lamb of God who takes away the sin of the world" (John 1:29). The terminal point for the prophets as the primary carriers of revelation seems to be identified by our Lord Himself. Matthew quotes Him to say, "For all the Prophets and the Law prophesied until John" (Matthew 11:13). Messiah Himself, whom the prophets foretold, inaugurated the climax of Biblical revelation and ushered in the Apostolic Epoch (Chapter Eight).

### Historical Overview: Prophetic Epoch

For a thousand years of Biblical history, from King David (c. 1000 B.C.) to King Jesus, the prophets were the primary messengers of redemptive revelation. Theirs was a period of general decline for Israel in loyalty and faithfulness to the God of their fathers. The prophets kept reminding Israel of the role to which they were called by God to serve as his faithful people through whom the promise of redemption would be realized. Israel in turn repeatedly forgot the special purpose for which they were chosen as God's special people.

The landmark events during the Prophetic Epoch include the following:

1. The Davidic monarchy establishing the redemptive line from Israel's greatest king till the coming of the Christ.

2. The Division of the Kingdom (931 B.C.) between the northern ten tribes (Israel) and the southern tribe of Judah. Since the tribe of Benjamin was virtually wiped out in inter-tribal warfare during the period of the Judges, it was no longer counted among the twelve (Judges 20 & 21).

3. The Assyrian Captivity and total destruction of the Northern Kingdom (721 B.C.).

4. The Babylonian Captivity of Judah (607 B.C.) known as the Exile, from which a remnant returned to resettle Judah (537 B.C.).

5. The rebuilding of the Temple at Jerusalem and restoration of the worship life of the faithful remnant who returned from exile in Babylon (537-505 B.C.).

6. Queen Esther's courageous appeal to Xerxes I, King of Persia, to prevent the planned annihilation of the Jews in the empire (c. 474 B.C.).

7. The reestablishment of the Mosaic Law (Civil, Ceremonial, Moral) under Ezra (c. 454 B.C.).

8. Nehemiah's effective leadership of the effort to rebuild the walls of Jerusalem (c. 444 B.C.).

9. The Birth of the Promised One, in whom all the promises of redemption were realized (c. 4 B.C.).

The Exile threatened a rupture in redemption history. It occurred near the mid-point of the Prophetic Epoch (607-537 B.C.). The prophets of the Old Testament are usually identified as Pre-Exilic, Exilic, and Post-Exilic depending on whether they prophesied before, during, or after the Captivity of Judah.

Pre-exilic prophets include Hosea, Isaiah, Amos, Micah, Jonah, Nahum, Zephaniah, Habbakkuk, and Jeremiah. Jeremiah served as a bridge person into the time of the Exile since he prophesied in Judah from 626 to 583 B.C. and witnessed the destruction of Jerusalem by the Chaldeans in 587 B.C.

Exilic prophets include Ezekiel and Daniel.

Post-exilic prophets include Haggai, Zechariah, and Malachi.

### The Prophets: God's Guardians of the Kingdom

The task of the prophets was to serve as guardians of the kingdom, God's agents to keep the kingdom a true representation of the rule of God among His people. For that reason they were frequently involved with the successive kings to exercise guardianship at the decision making centers of the kingdom. It was the kings who set the pattern of life for the people for good or ill, God or evil. As the kings went, so went the nation. For the sake of the nation the prophets addressed the kings with God's requirements. More correctly stated, the prophets understood the purpose for Israel's existence and therefore they called kings to accountability before God whose servants they should have recognized themselves to be. While intensely loyal to their nation, it was God's honor and His purposes for the nation which commanded their highest loyalty.

The issue of loyalty to God above all human authority distinguished the true prophets of the Lord from the multitude of false prophets. The false prophets were professionals who enjoyed official status in kings' courts. They were the "yes men" of government circles who lent a halo of sanctity to the political and military policies of the party in power (cf. I Kings 22:6). They spoke "flattering divinations" to their employer's satisfaction, speaking words they knew the people they served wanted to hear.

By contrast, the true prophets declared God's word regardless of the consequences to themselves or the embarrassment of the political establishment. Micah ridicules the prophets who sold comforting messages to those who could pay (Micah 3:5 & 11). Ezekiel speaks of prophets and prophetesses who practiced their profane prophetism "for a few handfuls of barley and scraps of bread" (Ezekiel 13:19). Compare this to Elisha's insistent refusal to accept pay in the form of Naaman's offered gifts, and the penalty inflicted upon his servant Gehazi for pursuing Naaman to request a reward (II Kings 5:19-27). There is never a suggestion that the true prophets ever took payment for services rendered. Amos was indignant when Amaziah, the professional pagan priest of Bethel, implied that Amos earned his living giving out oracles (Amos 7:12 & 13). The faithful prophets were God's spokespersons, accountable only to Him, independent of any compromising influence in their proclamation of God's word.

The intimacy of their relationship to God proved to be a costly privilege for the true prophets. They lived lives of isolation, rejection, and alienation, often persecuted by the very people whose spiritual welfare was their deep concern. Yet they remained with the people of God even when the people didn't live at all like God's people. As God's watchmen over the "house of Israel" their efforts were directed at making Israel a people fit for God's possession as agents to serve God's purposes in history. When Elijah tried to flee the country depressed over the refusal of the people to listen to God's word, he was stopped, reprimanded, and ordered back (I Kings 19:1-18). There was no escape from the calling to be a bearer of the word of the Lord. Jeremiah cursed the day of his birth in the agony of bearing in his own life the burden of God's grief over the sins of Judah (Jeremiah 20:14-18). The awesome responsibility of the faithful prophets could not be terminated by way of retirement or change of profession.

With the inescapability of declaring God's word came a convinced sense of unworthiness. Isaiah pronounces woe on himself as a person of unclean lips and heart (Isaiah 6:5). Jeremiah argues his unfitness as a prophet because he was not a persuasive speaker and was inexperienced for the task (Jeremiah 1:6). Arrogant pride and self confidence was absent from the prophets' demeanor. No celebrity mentality characterized their approach. Their first concern was that people should follow the Lord. They made no attempt to develop a personality cult of fawning followers. They never started their own religious organizations. Like the last of their kind, John the Baptist, the prophets' motto was "He must become greater; I must become less" (John 3:30). They spoke with power arising out of a deep dependence upon the One who sent them. Theirs also was the power of love, concern, and burden for people who, like erring children, didn't know that their best interest was to be found in the service of their Redeemer God.

### The Message of the Prophets

It may seem strange, or at least an over-simplification, to speak of the message of the prophets in the singular. We've already observed that the Prophetic Epoch covers a period of history from Samuel to John the Baptist, fully a thousand years. During that time scores of prophets served as God's spokespersons at varying stages of Old Testament history. The written accounts of their messages cover widely scattered time periods. Their styles differed as did the specific issues that were being addressed. And yet they shared in common an understanding of their God-given roles in the covenant community as well as the essential message which they were charged to bring. That message focused upon the relation of Israel to her God. Accordingly, all of the prophetic pronouncements included four major emphases. They reminded the people (1) who God is, (2) who they were, or were supposed to be, (3) what would

be the inevitable result if they refused to do God's will, and (4) tl
blessed consequences reserved for those faithful to the Lord. Let
summarize the essential teachings of the prophets on these fo
issues.

## Who the Lord Is

A teaching that stands out with unmistakable clarity in the prophe
is their insistence that there is one and only one God. In their pa
sion for the one and only true God they deny the existence of pagː
deities in sarcastic terms. The image representations of other goɩ
are ridiculed as the work of men's hands (Isaiah 2:8), manufacturɩ
gods falsely invested with deity (Hosea 14:3). Though representɩ
with hands, eyes, feet and other bodily features, they could n
speak, see, hear, move, or function in any way (Psalm 115:3-8
Hosea speaks of an idol as a "stick of wood" (Hosea 4:12). Amɩ
refers to suggestions that other gods are real deities as the pagan
lies (Amos 2:4).

In sharp contrast with the helpless, passive, non-existent pagɪ
gods, the God of the prophets is the active, living God. Amos esp
cially presents Jahweh as a God of creative action. He formed tl
mountains and created the wind, He made the stars, and tl
galaxies have the stamp of the divine arrangement. He set tl
bounds of the seas and pours water on the dry land (Amos 4:1
5:8). Isaiah's strong statements concerning God and the world iː
clude the metaphor of the potter and the clay, a great expressiɪ
figure of a sovereign God who takes the initiative in shaping tl
world and its history (Isaiah 29:16; 41:25; 64:8).

The great Creator Himself was the Redeemer of His people. Tl
prophets kept reminding Israel that the Sovereign Lord was the Gɩ
of their salvation. "But now, this is what the Lord says, he wl
created you, O Jacob, who formed you, O Israel: Fear not, for
have redeemed you; I have called you by name; you are minɩ
(Isaiah 43:1). Hosea warns his people of the futility of looking fɩ
salvation from any source except the Lord (Hosea 13:4). At tl
lowest point of despair in Judah's history, just before the collapɪ
of Jerusalem before Chaldea's might, Jeremiah calls God the "hoɪ
of Israel, its Savior in times of distress" (Jeremiah 14:8). Tl
prophets were convinced that however bleak the historical situatic
may appear, the God who stood above the affairs of people aɪ
nations would intervene as redeemer of those who trust Him. Othɩ

"gods" would disappear, forgotten forever when the nations which venerated them collapsed. Not so Israel's God. He was not dependent on Israel's fortunes and, therefore, was able to respond as Redeemer when Israel's sin imperilled her survival.

Jahweh is also the Covenant-keeping God according to the prophets. He remembered His promises made to the ancient forefathers. If it weren't for God's faithfulness, there would have been no hope for the survival of the unfaithful nation. Malachi 3:6 & 7 is to the point.

> I the Lord do not change. So you, O descendants of Jacob, are not destroyed. Ever since the time of your forefathers you have turned away from my decrees and have not kept them. Return to me, and I will return to you, says the Lord Almighty.

The changeless One guaranteed the continuation of the divine purpose of redemption even though the human partners in the drama were reduced to a small remnant of the faithful.

*Who Israel Is*

The prophet's concept of what constituted Israel's essential identity had little to do with a politically defined group or an ethnically identified tribe. Rather, their conviction concerning Israel had to do with their relation to God. True Israel was a people in fellowship with God, whose destiny was bound up completely in that relationship. They were not like other nations who were foreign to God's rule. Theirs was a unique, personal relationship with the God of heaven. Covenant, as the prophets understood it, was not primarily a legal contract but involved a deeply and intensely personal commitment. Like the marriage covenant, which was a frequent metaphor of the prophets, the personal commitment of love, loyalty, and trust was the essence without which the legal arrangement was meaningless. The inward reality of covenant they identified in terms of "hesedh," steadfast, enduring love. Breaking covenant, therefore, was not understood as mere contract violation but as infidelity.

Israel's special relationship with God goes back to the call of Abraham "To be my people" and a promise "to be your God" (cf. Isaiah 51:1 & 2). The prophets identified the confirmation of this promise with the deliverance of the enslaved descendants of Jacob from Egyptian bondage. Jeremiah refers to that event in "honeymoon" terms.

> I remember the devotion of your youth, how as a bride you loved me and followed me through the desert, through a land not sown. Israel was holy to the Lord, the firstfruits of his harvest (Jeremiah 2:2-3a).

Isaiah similarly speaks in marriage fidelity terms.

> For your Maker is your husband, the Lord Almighty is his name, the Holy One of Israel is your Redeemer, he is called the God of the whole earth.

> The Lord will call you back as if you were a wife deserted and distressed in spirit, a wife who married young, only to be rejected, says your God (Isaiah 54:5 & 6).

Conversely, whenever Israel was unfaithful to her heavenly Husband, the prophets chided her in terms suggestive of marriage infidelity and adultery. "Where is your mother's certificate of divorce," says Isaiah to a people who forsook their heavenly spouse and who married themselves to idols and the pursuit of evil (Isaiah 50:1). Hosea's parabolic identification of his disloyal wife Gomer with Israel was an unmistakable word of judgment against religious prostitution (Hosea 1:2; Hosea 3). Breaking covenant with the Lord was nothing short of adultery (Jeremiah 3:1; Jeremiah 23:10; Hosea 7:4; Ezekiel 23:45).

Both the prophet's view of the essential calling of Israel as a people and the intimacy of their relation with the Lord were reflected in and demonstrated by the names used for Israel. Isaiah lists three of them in one short statement; *servant, chosen, and friend.*

> But you, O Israel, my servant Jacob whom I have chosen, you descendants of Abraham my friend,

> I took you from the ends of the earth, from its farthest corners I called you. I said you are my servant I have chosen you and have not rejected you.

> So do not fear, for I am with you, do not be dismayed for I am your God (Isaiah 41:8-10).

The titles "chosen," "servant," and "friend" are supremely rich. To be the Lord's chosen implies a privileged status, not as an end in itself but as those whom God has graciously called to be His channel of blessing to the nations. "Servant" is also a title of honor since it means one who has been taken into the Lord's confidence, who knows and joyfully does the Master's will. And Israel addressed as God's corporate friend reminds them that the Lord's friendship with Abraham was intended to be perpetuated in his believing descendants.

Other designations for Israel in the prophets include "Called by my Name" and "portion" or "inheritance." These terms emphasized God's ownership of His people. They bore His Name. God's brand was burned into them. They were His treasured possession, His private property. He had laid claim to them to the point of risking His reputation before the nations with them (cf. Jeremiah 14:7-10; Zechariah 2:12; Isaiah 45:4; Daniel 9:19).

## The Consequences of Evil

So much of prophetic utterance was addressed against the evils within the covenant community that the prophet's writings tend to be identified primarily with declarations of judgment. Indeed, every faithful prophet challenged the people with the social injustices and religious wrongs that needed to be corrected. Theirs were reforming voices, urging redress of evils which corrupted the communal and political life of the nation. Their warnings were spoken out of hearts broken by the ungrateful waywardness of the people. The prophets' reaction was one of shock and amazement that a people so favored of the Lord would grieve their gracious God with calloused wickedness. Jeremiah is typical:

> Cross over to the coasts of Kittim and look, send to Kedar and observe closely; see if there has ever been anything like this. Has a nation ever changed its gods? (yet they are not gods at all.) But my people have exchanged their Glory for worthless idols.

> Be appalled at this O heavens, and shudder with great horror, declares the Lord. My people have committed two sins: They have forsaken me the fountain of living water and have dug cisterns, broken cisterns that cannot hold water (Jeremiah 2:10-13).

It is not difficult to understand why the prophets were so flabbergasted by the persistent drift toward moral and religious wickedness. The God of heaven had lavished His love upon them in unmistakable ways. His mercy and grace had been demonstrated in His special care over them and their forefathers ever since Abraham was called out of Ur. The Lord delivered them from Egyptian bondage, preserved them in the bleak wilderness, brought them into a verdant land, gave them the law, and the temple symbolized his perpetual presence among them. From among the families of the nations they had been chosen as God's "peculiar" people in that they were God's hand-picked partners to serve as a model for the nations. Through them the divine blessings for the world were intended to flow. They were privileged to be the channel for the Messiah, the Savior of the world. No more lofty calling could have been given. They had a purpose for their existence that embraced the world.

Why would a people habitually offend and grieve the Lord who was the source of their favored position?

One of the reasons for the constant drift toward wickedness was simple complacency. The prophets frequently warned against a casual attitude toward God and His commandments. Israel tended to take the Lord for granted as a guarantee against any misfortune. "Is not the Lord among us? No disaster will come upon us" (Micah 3:11). So certain were they that God would not punish or forsake them that they thought they could live as they pleased. After all, they were the promised people, inheritors of the promise to Abraham that they would be a blessing to all nations. God would have to preserve them or go back on His word. That would be an impossibility. If they were destroyed, God would have no agency for fulfilling His word.

Since the Lord had intervened so often in their history as the Deliverer of His people, Israel thought itself immune to destruction. Past actions of grace were interpreted as insurance policies for the future. Promises made to Abraham and Moses and David were thought to insure their security. Since Jahweh had bound Himself to Israel they thought they were indispensible to the divine plan. Besides, the temple was there as a reminder of God's presence among them. Their conclusion was "Disaster will not overtake or meet us" (Amos 9:10). Through Jeremiah, the Lord makes clear what He thinks of such an attitude.

> Will you steal and murder, commit adultery and perjury, burn incense to Baal and follow other gods you have not known, And then come and stand before me in this house which bears my Name and say "We are safe - safe to do all these detestable things? Has this house, which bears my Name, become a den of robbers to you? But I have been watching! Declares the Lord." (Jeremiah 7:9-11)

The prophets insistently reminded their people that privilege required responsibility. "You only have I chosen of all the families of the earth; therefore I will punish you for all your sins" (Amos 3:2). Irresponsibility, complacency, and evil cost the majority their favored status with the Lord and resulted in the destruction of their nation and its capital Jerusalem by the army of Nebuchadnezzer (587 B.C.). A pagan nation was the instrument of God's discipline of His chosen people. The Exile was the means by which God punished an ungrateful people who insisted on deviating from God's will as the prophets proclaimed it. It served to purify idolatry from the national life but at the cost of near annihilation of the nation. Only a small remnant survived to serve as partners with God to further His plan of salvation.

A second reason that made Israel such easy prey for wicked behavior was greed. The acquisitive desire for material possessions is deeply ingrained in the human heart. The lure of wealth was often a corrupting attraction in the Israel of the prophets.

> From the least to the greatest all are greedy for gain; prophets and priests alike all practice deceit. (Jeremiah 6:13)

> Her leaders judge for a bribe, her priests teach for a price, and her prophets tell fortunes for money. Yet they lean upon the Lord and say, "Is not the Lord among us? No disaster will come upon us." (Micah 3:11)

Greed and material gain also lay at the base of most *religious* apostasy. The driving motive toward idolatry, especially Baal worship, was the promise of abundant crops, enlarged herds, and healthy children. Baal was the god of fertility, reproduction, and sex potential. Baal and his many Baalim (lesser gods) were credited with the production of the fields and reproduction of cattle and the birth of children. The repulsive practice of temple prostitution was an expected consequence of religious belief in fertility cults. If Baal was the "divine" power behind all reproduction, then the sex act with a temple prostitute before the pagan shrine was a "sacrament" by which one could approach closest to the "divine" in reality. The sacrifice of children on the fiery altars of the Ammonite god Molech followed the same distorted belief pattern. Molech was the god who was presumed to have been the source of the fertility responsible for the child's birth. Sacrificing the first born child was intended to assure continued reproductive fertility from its "divine" source. Additional children could be guaranteed only if the first child was sacrificed to the god of reproduction.

Israel and Judah assumed that they were guaranteed Jahweh's favor. In addition, they thought they could also tap whatever benefits could be gained by the worship of others gods. Greedy for abundant crops, increasing herds, and enlarged numbers of children, they adopted pagan cult practices thinking thereby to enlarge their possessions. The prophets never ceased pronouncing the judgment of the Lord against this religious eclecticism. Hosea uses the metaphor "lovers" to identify Israel's infatuation with fertility gods:

> She said, I will go after my lovers, who give me my food and my water, my wool and my linen, my oil and my drink.
>
> She has not acknowledged that I was the one who gave her the grain, the new wine and oil, who lavished on her the silver and the gold which they used for Baal.
>
> I will ruin her vines and her fig trees, which she said were her pay from her lovers.
>
> I will make them a thicket and wild animals will devour them. I will punish her for the days she burned incense to the Baals (Hosea 2:5,8,12,13a).

King Solomon, David's own son, carries the greatest responsibility for introducing idolatry to Israel. He provided pagan temples and shrines for his many foreign wives to continue their idolatrous practices.

> On a hill east of Jerusalem, Solomon built a high place for Chemosh the detestable god of Moab, and for Molech the detestable god of the Ammonites. He did the same for all his foreign wives, who burned incense and offered sacrifices to their gods (I Kings 11:7 & 8).

The presence of pagan religious institutions served to make Israel familiar with false belief systems and practices. They became accustomed to foreign religions which very soon seemed attractive. After Solomon's death (931 B.C.) the kingdom was divided north (Israel) and south (Judah). Following Jeroboam's lead, the northern kingdom turned completely to paganism. The southern kingdom, led by descendants of David as its kings, held out somewhat longer before following the same fatal practices. The prophets unanimously identified idolatry as the single greatest evil for which Israel was punished with captivity to Assyria (721 B.C.) and Judah was reduced to slavery in Babylonian captivity after the destruction of Jerusalem (587 B.C.).

The inevitable judgment of the Lord against evil was rooted in divine love and grace. His people had to be jarred out of their complacent wickedness in order to repent and turn to Him who alone was the source of blessing. The Lord disciplined His people to prevent their total surrender to self-destructive sin. The salvation of the world depended upon the survival of at least a faithful minority through whom the world's Redeemer would be revealed. Whom the Lord loved He rebuked through His servants, the prophets. Their messages of disaster ahead for a disobedient people were intended to confront them with the reality of their responsibility to the living God in their own time. Sin threatened to disqualify them for serving as co-workers with the Lord in fulfilling the divine purpose in history.

### The Rewards of Righteousness

In spite of all of their pronouncements of judgment on a rebellious people, the prophets were not pessimists. They knew that Jahweh was a promise-keeping God. He had promised that, through the descendants of Abraham, blessings would accrue to the whole world. He had chosen Israel as the means by which all nations would be blessed. His promised Messiah, eventually born of this people, would be the Messenger of grace and salvation for believers to the ends of the earth. The message of the prophets is fundamentally a message of hope because their confidence was in the integrity and faithfulness of the Unchanging One.

There is good news in the prophets. While they agonized in sympathetic pain when harsh words of discipline had to be spoken from the Lord, the warmth of compassion filled their words of promise.

> Who is a God like you, who pardons sin and forgives the transgression of the remnant of his inheritance?
>
> You do not stay angry forever but delight to show mercy.
>
> You will again have compassion on us; you will tread our sins underfoot and hurl all our iniquities into the depths of the sea.
>
> You will be true to Jacob, and show mercy to Abraham, as you pledged an oath to our fathers in days long ago. (Micah 7:18-20)

Hosea uses what is perhaps the strongest language to describe the judgments of the Lord awaiting those who "offer human sacrifices and kiss the calf-idols" (Hosea 13:2). Yet the last chapter of his prophecy opens with an impassioned call to repentance.

> Return, O Israel, to the Lord your God. Your sins have been your downfall. Take words with you and return to the Lord. Say to him: Forgive all our sins and receive us graciously, that we may offer the fruit of our lips.
>
> We will never again say "Our gods" to what our own hands have made, for in you the fatherless find compassion (Hosea 14:1-3).

Even in the worst of times, just before Jerusalem was sacked and plundered by the Chaldean army, Jeremiah announced eventual restoration from captivity for a faithful remnant.

> This is what the Lord says: "When seventy years are completed for Babylon, I will come to you and bring you back to this place. For I know the plans I have for you," declares the Lord, "plans to prosper you and not to harm you, plans to give you a hope and a future. Then you will call upon me and come and pray to me, and I will listen to you. You will seek me and find me when you seek me with all your heart" (Jeremiah 29:10-13).

## From Exile to Christ

### Exilic Prophets: Ezekiel and Daniel

While in Exile (607-537 B.C.), the people of Judah were not forsaken by their Covenant God, who, through his prophets Ezekiel and Daniel, promised deliverance and restoration to the repentant faithful.

Ezekiel went into captivity with the second deportation in 597 B.C. and continued to prophesy until 570 B.C. Although most of his book focuses attention on God's justice in punishing Judah and the nations for their sin, the certainty of Judah's restoration is also emphasized. Ezekiel never lived to personally witness the fulfillment of his own prophecies, but lived and died in hope that a mighty act of God would restore the fortunes of Zion.

A crucial passage, summarizing the causes for the exile, and the Lord's determination to deliver a remnant from captivity is Ezekiel 36:16-32. Verses 16-21 recount Judah's misdeeds, covenant disloyalty, and how she brought shame upon the God who had called her to be his own possession. She discredited the name of Jahweh and received the just consequences of her sins. Nevertheless, God's name would be vindicated by Judah's restoration to the land promised to her forefathers, in spite of Judah's unworthiness.

Ezekial 36:22-32 is a prophecy of God's gracious initiative which will assure deliverance from captivity: He will gather them from the nations; He will bring them into their own land (vs. 24); He will cleanse them from idolatry (vs. 25); He will put a new spirit within them (vs. 26); He will restore them to obedience (vs. 27); He will reestablish the covenant (vs. 28).

So again we have a renewal of the covenant, with God as "party of the first part" assuming obligations and promises and Judah as "part of the second part" called to repentance (vs. 31 & 32) and obedience (vs. 27).

Daniel went into exile with the first deportation about 607 B.C. He was likely a very young man at the time, showed promise of great intelligence, and was, according to Josephus, a relative of king Zedekiah who was the king in Jerusalem at the time of its destruction in 587 B.C. Daniel was destined for a successful career as advisor to emperors. His life in Babylon extended from the first year of Nebuchadnezzar, through five succeeding Chaldean kings' reigns, past the fall of Babylon (539 B.C.), until the third year of Cyrus' reign (536 B.C.). In all, Daniel was God's spokesman beginning with the early years of Captivity and continuing for a total of 72 years. He was God's witness in the court of the most powerful monarchs in the world during one of the most crucial periods in Revelational history. His prophetic visions consist of sweeping accounts of historical events culminating in the coming of the Messiah (chapter 9) and in the consummation of the Second

Coming (chapter 2). His trust in Jawheh as the God of history was not shaken by the circumstances of the Captivity. (cf. Daniel 6:29)

## A Faithful Remnant Returns

The historical books of Ezra, Nehemiah, and Esther present covenant history beginning with the original return from Captivity until Jerusalem was rebuilt. These books demonstrate how faithful covenant partners, called to do God's will, play important roles in God's plan to save the world through the coming of Christ. The major historical events during the first 100 years after the exile should be kept in mind when reading these books.

539 B.C. - Babylon fell to Persian might.

538 B.C. - Cyrus, King of Persia, decreed that those Jews who wished could return to resettle Judah and rebuild the Temple.

537 B.C. - The first group to return departed for Judah and began rebuilding the Temple under Haggai, Zechariah, (prophets) Joshua, son of Josedeck (priest) and Zerubbabel (governor).

515 B.C. - The temple was restored and the worship life of the covenant people reestablished (Zechariah 1:16).

477 B.C. - Esther became queen of Persia, wife of Ahasuerus (his Persian name was Xerxes I 486-465 B.C.). Her intercession with the King prevented the annihilation of the Jews (Esther 7).

454 B.C. - Ezra led a second group of returning exiles and led a revival of the Mosaic Law as determinative for the life of the covenant community (Nehemiah 8).

444 B.C. - Nehemiah led a third group of exiles from Babylon to join the settlers who were already there. The walls of Jerusalem were completed under his leadership (Nehemiah 4-6).

Thus the return from the Exile was a process, rather than a single event, covering nearly a century of Israel's history. Ezra, Nehemiah, and Esther are, therefore, accounts of very significant revelational events which assure the continuity of the covenant moving toward its fullest realization in the coming of Jesus Christ.

Although Esther comes after Ezra and Nehemiah in the Biblical order, the events recorded in the book of Esther (c. 475 B.C.) predate Ezra by about twenty years and Nehemiah by nearly forty years. We can only speculate what might have happened to the struggling Jewish immigrants in Judah had Esther not been faithful at her providential moment of responsibility. Jerusalem might never have been rebuilt had it not been for Esther's efforts, and subsequent history would have been significantly altered.

In any event, Esther's marriage to Xerxes I and her willingness to risk her queenly privileges for the sake of her people, assured the survival of the Jews in Persia. Many of these surviving Jews accompanied Ezra and Nehemiah to Jerusalem, joining with those who were already there to rebuild the city walls. Together they participated in the reestablishment of a formal covenant community through whom the world's Savior would be revealed several hundred years later. As always, covenant faithfulness involved a conscious awareness of God's dealings with His people in the past, and the realization that the future is shaped by the measure of responsibility God's people exercise in their own time.

Artaxerxes (465-424 B.C.) succeeded his father Xerxes to the Persian throne. It was Artaxerxes who commissioned Nehemiah to return to Jerusalem to supervise the rebuilding of Jerusalem's walls (Nehemiah 2). It was very unusual to allow a conquered nation to rebuild the walls of its capital city. Walls represented military defense and, therefore, constituted a threat to the conqueror's rule. Why would Artaxerxes allow the Jews to rebuild Jerusalem's walls?

It is likely that Esther, the second wife of Xerxes, became the step-mother of Artaxerxes. It is not too much to speculate that she taught him something of the history of the Jewish people. This influence could very likely account for the kindly disposition Artaxerxes had toward the Jews after he became the Persian emperor. Certainly the Lord's providence often works through intimate personal relations. After all, Pharoah's daughter was used as a step-mother to preserve Moses for leadership at the time of Israel's birth as a nation. Perhaps the Jewish step-mother of a future Persian emperor was influential in making the restoration of Jerusalem's walls possible after the Exile.

## Post-Exilic Prophets--Haggai and Zechariah

After the exile, the prophets of Judah continued to proclaim God's word for His covenant people, anticipating the approaching fulfillment of the Promise of a coming Savior.

Haggai the Prophet was an older contemporary of Zechariah, and may have been old enough to have seen the original temple of Solomon before its destruction in 587 B.C.

Haggai was burdened for the rebuilding of the Temple by the returning exiles. The foundation was laid in 536 B.C. soon after the return of the exiles, but sixteen years later the superstructure was not yet completed. The people were busy building their own paneled bi-levels, failing to "seek first God's kingdom" (1:3). They were not prospered in their own endeavors because they were unfaithful toward God's work represented by an unfinished Temple (1:5-11). Haggai insisted that economic stress, unemployment, and drought were directly traceable to neglect in building the Temple. Their repentant response under Joshua (High Priest), Zerubbabel (governor or king), and Haggai (prophet) resulted in resuming the work of Temple building (1:12-15).

The Temple, especially the Holy of Holies, was so significant because it represented God's presence among his people and symbolized their religious unity. Other nations needed kings' courts to constitute themselves a political unity. Not so Israel. They were a Covenant people whose true character was determined by their relationship to God. The Temple as the dwelling place of God and the center of the worship life of His people was the most important structure in the land. To neglect its construction was a faithless act, rejecting the theocentric character of themselves as the people of the Lord.

Future references in Haggai include the prophecy of 2:6-9 that "in a little while" God will shake the heavens and earth, which Hebrews 12:24-29 links with the new covenant in Christ and the Messianic Kingdom He would establish. The glory of Haggai's Temple is seen in that it is a link between Solomon's Temple and the Messiah, God in person dwelling among his people.

Zechariah saw the Temple building brought to its conclusion, and the reestablishment of the temple service, which included morning and evening sacrifices and all the special rites associated with the various feasts.

Zechariah 1:1-6 is especially to the point. The prophet seems to say, "Don't make the mistake your forefathers made, who disregarded the prophets' warnings in their time and ended up in captivity. Learn from their rebellious error, and be obedient to the word of the Lord in your time. Only then will you serve as the agency in God's hand to bring salvation to the nations through the coming Savior."

## Conclusion: Prophetic Epoch

The long ages stretching from David to Christ, fully a thousand years, represent a troubled era of Biblical history. Repeatedly God demonstrated his faithful determination to complete the plan of redemption in spite of human vacillation. By the time of Jesus' birth, very few people were eager anticipators of the fulfillment of God's promise. There was just a small group of shepherds on a Judean hillside, a few wise men from distant lands, Simeon and Anna prayerfully waiting in Temple service, and, of course, Joseph and Mary, step-father and virgin mother of the world's Savior. But a faithful God remembered His promises and the climax of salvation history was reached, the Seed of Promise was born.

## Discussion Stimulators, Chapter Seven

1. Review the "landmark events" in Bible history during the Prophetic Epoch.

2. I Kings 22 presents two radically different kinds of prophets in its account. It contrasts the professional court-prophets in the service of a king with the independence of a true prophet accountable only to the Lord. Review this chapter highlighting the areas of contrast.

3. What were some of the distinguishing characteristics of the true prophets?

4. From the review of the message of the prophets identify what they proclaimed about who God was, who Israel and Judah were, what the consequences of evil were and what the rewards of righteousness would be.

5. What reasons can be given for the repeated drift toward idolatry and general wickedness in spite of God's kindness and love toward the people of Israel? Are the same dangers present in the Christian community today?

6. What made the Exile such a crucial juncture in Old Testament history? What were some of the results of the Exile?

## For Further Study

Achtemeier, Paul and Elizabeth, *The Old Testament Roots of Our Faith,* (Nashville, Abingdom, 1962).

De Graaf, S.G., *Promise and Deliverance,* (St. Catherines, Ont., Paideia Press, 1977) II.

Ellison, H. L., *The Prophets of Israel,* (Grand Rapids, Eerdmans, 1969).

Halley, H. H., *Bible Handbook,* (Grand Rapids, Zondervan, 1965) pp. 285-401.

Lewis, J. P., *The Minor Prophets,* (Grand Rapids, Baker, 1980).

Schaeffer, F., *Death in the City,* (Downers Grove, IVF, 1980).

Stedman, R.C., *Death of a Nation,* (Waco, Word, 1976).

Von Orelli, C., "Prophecy," *International Standard Bible Encyclopedia,* ed. James Orr (Grand Rapids, Eerdmans, 1949) IV, 2459-2466.

Vos, G., *Biblical Theology,* (Grand Rapids, Eerdmans, 1948) Part Two.

# The Apostolic Epoch of Biblical Revelation

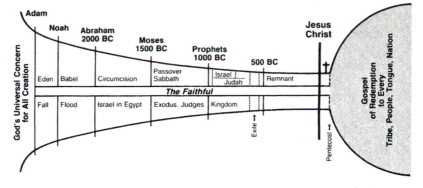

I. Christ Fulfilled Old Testament Scripture.

II. Christ Guarantees Old Testament Promises.

    A. Adamic Epoch.

        1. Christ the Second Adam.

        2. Christ was Victor Over Demonic Evil.

    B. Noahic Epoch.

        1. The Flood, a Warning for Every Age.

        2. Japheth's Descendants Will Follow Seth's God.

        3. The Curse of Canaan Reversed by Christ.

        4. The Tower of Babel Reversed in Pentecost.

    C. Abrahamic Epoch.

        1. Abraham, Father of All Believers.

        2. The Privilege of Being a Jew.

        3. Circumcision as Covenant Sign.

        4. The Land of Canaan as Eternal Possession.

    D. Mosaic Epoch.

        1. Christ Fulfilled Moses' Testimony.

        2. Christ Fulfilled the Law.

        3. Passover Anticipated Holy Communion.

        4. Sabbath Anticipated Sunday.

        5. Christ, the Perfect Atonement for Sin.

    E. Prophetic Epoch.

        1. The Kingly Messiah.

        2. Messiah as Suffering Servant.

# The Apostolic Epoch of Biblical Revelation

THE Prophetic Epoch was not the last chapter in God's design for his chosen people. If that had been the case the message of the Old Testament would end on a rather depressing note. The glorious future envisioned by the Prophets for the people of God could hardly be identified with the remnant who returned from exile to resettle Jerusalem and environs. Yes, the exile appeared to cure them of the tendency toward idolatry. But apart from that one positive feature, the life of the community to which Malachi prophesied after the exile differed little from the pattern that prevailed before the exile. He spoke God's word of judgment against insincere worship, greedy priests, easy divorce, adultery, perjury, and injustice to the poor, the widows, and the orphans. This hardly describes a people who fulfilled the promise to the Patriarchs that their descendants would be a blessing to the nations. The true fulfillment of Old Testament revelation awaited the Apostolic Epoch and beyond.

We refer to the Revelation given in the New Testament as "Apostolic" because the apostles were the messengers of the divine revelation contained therein. They were the source for the content of the New Testament Scriptures and, in many cases, the actual writers themselves. But while the apostles were the divinely chosen agents of the revelation, the central concern of New Testament truth is the Person and work of the Lord Jesus Christ. Not only is He the focus of the light of the New Testament but He is revealed as the culmination and fulfillment of the promises and hopes of the Old Testament. We cannot understand the Old Testament without the New nor the New Testament separated from the Old. Together they constitute one message which centers upon Jesus Christ, the Messiah, the incarnate Son of God.

## Christ Fulfills Old Testament Scripture

Repeatedly we are thrust back to the Old Testament to understand the message of Christ in the New. Consider Hebrews 1:1-3.

> In the past God spoke to our forefathers through the prophets at many times and in various ways, but in these last days he has spoken to us by his Son, whom he appointed heir of all things and through whom he made the universe. The Son is the radiance of God's glory and the exact representation of his being, sustaining all things by his powerful word. After he had provided purification for sins, he sat down at the right hand of the Majesty in heaven.

What a sweeping introduction to this epistle about Jesus! It draws us back to the prophets and before them to the original creation to tell us who Jesus is and what he has done. The rest of the book demonstrates how Jesus Christ is everything the books of Moses and the prophets said the Messiah would be. He is the one descendant of Abraham who did the will of His Heavenly Father in perfection (Hebrews 2:14-18). He is the perfect High Priest, of which the priests of Israel were imperfect shadows (Hebrews 7:26-28). He is the perfect sacrificial Lamb offered once for all, of which the repeated offerings under the old order were temporary types of the ultimate offering to come (Hebrews 9:26-28). He is the "new and living way" through whom the believer enters the holy of holies, the presence of God Himself (Hebrews 9:11-14). The many Old Testament figures listed in Hebrews 11 are described as living by faith in anticipation of the redemption to come, "whose architect and builder is God" (Hebrews 11:10). As the temple was the center of the worship life of the old order, so Christ is the Living Temple and the worship of God is now centered in Him.

All the apostolic writings of the New Testament bear witness to this common theme, namely the continuity between all epochs of revelation and Jesus Christ as the culminating revelational event. Consider how the very first sentence in the New Testament draws it all together. Matthew writes, "A record of the genealogy of Jesus Christ, the Son of David, the Son of Abraham." In order to tell his readers about the meaning of Jesus' birth, Matthew reaches back a thousand years to David, and two thousand years to Abraham. Only then can he explain the momentous nature and significance of Jesus' birth.

The apostle John begins his gospel of the public ministry of Jesus by identifying Him as the living Word who was with the Father from eternity.

> In the beginning was the Word and the Word was with God, and the Word was God (John 1:1).

> The Word became flesh and lived for awhile among us. We have seen his glory, the glory of the one and only Son who came from the Father, full of grace and truth (John 1:14).

The apostle's use of the term "Word" is extremely significant. The primary and most efficient way in which persons can communicate with each other is through the use of words. Thus the personal God of heaven communicated His will through spoken and written words to Adam, Noah, Abraham, Moses, and many others. But when the Son of God appeared in person, then the perfect and final divine communication had taken place. He was the final and ultimate Word, the best possible communication from the Heavenly Father. "Anyone who has seen me has seen the Father," said Jesus to his questioning disciple, Philip (John 14:9). The fullest revelation of the Father's will is seen in the Person and work of the divine Son. He is, therefore, *the* Word in the flesh, to which all other scriptural words point for their understanding.

John the Baptist, as a herald trumpeting the arrival of a king, identified himself as a "voice crying in the desert; make straight the way of the Lord" (John 1:23). Isaiah had said that such a public announcement would precede the event when "the glory of the Lord will be revealed" (Isaiah 40:5). In style and power like Elijah, John proclaimed Jesus "the Lamb of God" (Malachi 4:5; John 1:36). As the last of a long line of prophets, John witnessed and declared the arrival of the One whom all the faithful prophets had anticipated. He said, "I have seen and testify that this is the Son of God" (John 1:34).

The Gospel of Luke records Jesus' own testimony concerning Himself as the culmination of Old Testament revelation.

> Jesus took the Twelve aside and told them, "How foolish you are, and how slow of heart to believe all that the prophets had spoken! Did not the Christ have to suffer these things then enter his glory?" And beginning with Moses and all the Prophets, he explained to them what was said in all the Scriptures concerning himself (Luke 24:25-27).

### Christ Guarantees Old Testament Promises

If Jesus is indeed the culmination of the hopes and promises of Old Testament revelation, we should be able to discover specific references of this fact in the record of the New Testament. In fact, the writings of the apostles should be tested and interpreted in this light. We will only address a few of the major themes from each of the Epochs previously covered. But these, we trust, will demonstrate how Jesus Christ is the focus of the light of all Biblical revelation.

### Adamic Epoch

1. *Jesus Christ, the Second Adam.* In chapter three we observed that human beings were created to live in happy and joyful fellowship with their God. A perfect world which provided everything necessary for life and well-being was at their disposal. Their responsibility was to be ruling stewards of the creation to develop its potential in praise of the Creator. But Adam and Eve refused to serve as spokespersons for the creation in obedient dependence upon God. Instead, they stubbornly insisted upon doing their own will, attempting to find fulfillment in life independent of Him who is the Source of all that enriches life. Lured by the tempting prospect of self-gratification they fell from the lofty position as companion friends of God and plunged themselves and the human race into the futility of evil.

In contrast with the rebellious disobedience of the first Adam stands the faithful obedience of the Second Adam, Jesus Christ. Where Adam failed to be an obedient son, Christ prevailed. "For I have come down from heaven," said Jesus, "not to do my will but to do the will of Him who sent me" (John 6:38). His agonizing prayer in the garden of Gethsemane concluded with the words, "Yet not as I will but as you will" (Matthew 26:39). While the first Adam failed his probationary test of obedience so that the futility of death ruled all human endeavor to follow, so the obedience of the divine Son brings the reward of life. "For as in Adam all die, so all in Christ will be made alive" (I Corinthians 15:22). He is "the last Adam, a life-giving spirit" (I Corinthians 15:46). The exaltation of our Lord to the right hand of heavenly Majesty (Hebrews 1:3) was a reward for his obedience.

And being found in appearance as a man, he humbled himself and became obedient unto death - even death on a cross! Therefore, God exalted him to the highest place and gave him the name that is above every name, That at the name of Jesus every name shall bow, in heaven and on earth and under the earth and every tongue confess that Jesus Christ is Lord, to the glory of God the Father (Philippians 2:8-11).

Jesus' perfect life of obedience was so very important because only a perfect representative could serve as Savior for a lost humanity. From Adam, the first representative human, a flawed human race resulted. What was needed was a second representative human from whom perfect righteousness could be inherited (Romans 5:12-20). Christ alone meets this requirement so that the apostle Paul can write "we shall be saved through his life" (Romans 5:10).

Evangelical Christianity tends to focus almost exclusively on the death of Christ on the cross as the guarantee of salvation. Liberalism emphasizes Christ as the model human, the example for godly living. Both positions represent a one-sided emphasis. Jesus lived the perfect life of obedience which humans were created to do but didn't, and then died the perfect death to pay the penalty for the guilty. Without His perfect life his death would not have merited salvation for the lost. He would have had to die for His own sin. The total life of Christ, from humble birth to victorious resurrection, is the guarantee of salvation for those who identify by faith with Him. Because Christ was the sinless "seed of the woman" (Genesis 3:15) He could crush the head of the serpent and triumphed over the powers of darkness through his death and resurrection.

2. *Jesus Christ, Victor Over Demonic Evil.* Christ's victory over demonic temptation (Luke 4:1-13) stands as the reversal of the cowardly surrender to temptation in the garden of Eden. The devil's strategy in both instances was the same, namely, to attack at precisely those points of greatest human vulnerability. The apostle John details the three areas of human weakness in terms of lust, or soul-destroying cravings (I John 2:15 & 16). There is a fleshly lust or appeal through the craving of appetite, visual lust, or attractions through what is seen, and prideful lust, or the craving for prestige, recognition, and celebrity status. All three lustful avenues of temptation are addressed in the Genesis account of the Fall.

> When the woman saw that the fruit of the tree was good for food (fleshly craving) and pleasing to the eye (visual attraction) and also desirable for gaining wisdom (prideful lust) she took some and ate it. She also gave some to her husband and he ate it (Genesis 3:6).

Compare this account to the devil's approach to Jesus after His forty-day fast in the desert.

> If you are the Son of God tell this stone to become bread (fleshly craving) (Luke 4:3).

> The devil...showed him all the Kingdoms of the world. And he said to him, "I will give you all their authority and splendor...if you worship me it will all be yours." (visual lust) (Luke 4:5-7).

> If you are the Son of God, throw yourself down (prideful lust, challenging God to rescue him) (Luke 4:9).

In each case the devil's strategy was the same. It was a strategy that was always so successful. Even great figures in Bible history succumbed to the devil's efforts. There was Noah who became drunk with wine (fleshly cravings), and David who coveted Bathesheba, his neighbor's wife (visual lust), and numbered the people to see how powerful a monarch he was (prideful lust).

Human beings had always been so defenseless, so vulnerable before the Devil's efforts. No one, from Adam onward, was ever a match for the devil until Jesus triumphed over the evil one. He sent the powers of darkness retreating. Where Adam failed, Christ prevailed, as will all those and only those who look to Him for strength and grace. They share His victory and He triumphs anew in their victories over temptation.

The miracles our Lord also forcefully established the superiority of the Kingdom of God over the kingdom of evil. He healed the sick, raised the dead, broke the hold of demonic power over people's lives, stilled the troubled seas, all of which reversed the effects of the Fall. Once Jesus arrived on the human scene we are assured that God is in command, not the forces of evil which seemed so dominant before. Jesus claimed this world as the true King's Domain, the Kingdom of God, having wrestled it out of the hands of its demonic usurper. The victory is not yet complete but the issue is no longer in doubt. One final revelational act remains, the return in glory of our Lord, whereupon the kingdoms of this world shall have become the Kingdom of God and of His Christ, and He shall reign forever and ever (Revelation 11:15).

## Noahic Epoch

1. *The Flood, a warning for every age.* There are, in the New Testament apostolic writings, few references to the fulfillment of events and promises originating during the Noahic Epoch. Yet they ·are not entirely lacking. Matthew quotes Jesus comparing the indifference of the majority of the people to Noah's warnings in his day with the general attitude that will prevail before the Second Coming. Most people then and will again be so wrapped up in the pursuit of day-to-day concerns to the neglect of their accountability to God's Word which affects their eternal welfare. The Flood, therefore, stands as a reminder of the need for watchfulness and preparedness in anticipation of the coming of our Lord in glory.

> As it was in the days of Noah, so it will be at the coming of the Son of Man. For in the days before the flood, people were eating and drinking, marrying and giving in marriage, up to the day Noah entered the ark; and they knew nothing about what would happen until the flood came and took them all away. That is how it will be at the coming of the Son of Man (Matthew 24:37-39).

2. *Japheth's descendants will follow the God of Shem.* Noah's prophecy relating to his son Japheth has a direct bearing on the progressive unfolding of redemption history.

> May God extend the territory of Japheth; may Japheth live in the tents of Shem, and may Canaan be his slave (Genesis 9:27).

Previously (Genesis 9:26) Noah had exclaimed, "Blessed be the Lord, the God of Shem." This is not said of either of his other two sons, which indicates a special relation between the Lord and Shemites. They were the elected bearers of revelation and redemption. Later revelation confirms this because Abraham, David, and the Israelites were Shemites, to whom the true God revealed Himself and called them to be His purposeful partners. Since Jesus was a Shemite, Noah's statement, "Blessed be the God of Shem", has as its New Testament equivalent, "Blessed be the God and Father of our Lord Jesus Christ" (I Peter 1:3).

The phrase, "may Japheth live in the tents of Shem," anticipates a time when descendants of Japheth would overrun and conquer the Middle Eastern lands of the Shemites. Ultimately such conquest would introduce the Japhethites to the true God, the God of Shem, and therefore, serve as a great spiritual blessing to an enlarged portion of humanity. This prophecy, both as to its territorial import and its ultimate spiritual consequences, was fulfilled when first the Greeks and then the Romans controlled Middle Eastern Shemitic territory. These Japhethites conquered the "tents" or dwelling-places of Shemites, and in turn were introduced to the God of Shem. In God's providence this proved to be a blessing for the whole world. The Greek language and Roman efficiency in government and transport became potent factors in the spread of the Gospel to non-Shemite lands after the coming of Christ.

3. *The Curse of Canaan Reversed by Christ.* Seen in the light of eventual inclusion of the world's peoples in the blessings of the true religion, the Hamitic curse appears to have a temporary application. As a consequence of Ham's disrespect for his father, Ham's descendants, through his son Canaan, were consigned to servitude to the descendants of Ham's brothers, Shem and Japheth (Genesis 9:20-27). There was no promise at that point in salvation history that Ham's descendants would share in the blessings of "the God of Shem." But by the time of Abraham, who was a Shemite, the promise was enlarged to embrace *all* families of the earth, Ham's descendants included. This looks forward to a time when "the earth shall be full of the knowledge of the Lord as the waters cover the sea" (Isaiah 11:9). When, eventually, all the world's people would share equally the knowledge of the true God, there would be no place for privileged status and its attendant servitude of the less privileged. Equality before the Lord as participants in promised salvation precludes enslavement of any people. The redemption in Christ has as its intent the healing of all curses, including the Hamitic.

4. *The Tower of Babel Reversed in Pentecost.* Another revelational event from the Noahic Epoch which has its counterpoint in the Apostolic Epoch is the Tower of Babel incident (Genesis 11:1-9). Babel was essentially a revolt against heaven. United in common opposition to God, they erected a temple tower to symbolize their unity in rebellion. Divine intervention confused their language, forcing a dispersal of people to scattered areas organized around similarity of language.

Pentecost was the reverse of Babel (Acts 2:1-41). At Babel the confusion of language prevented people from understanding each other and forced them to scatter. At Pentecost scattered peoples from many lands came together and understood the apostle's message as the language of the gospel broke through human language diversity by the power of the Holy Spirit. Babel attempted unity through sinful human effort and caused disharmony. Pentecost brought unity in the Holy Spirit and shared fellowship in the family of God for people from all families of the earth. The fulfillment of Jesus' promise to send the Holy Spirit was a promise to heal sin-caused brokenness between the peoples of earth. Our relationship with Jesus Christ through the Holy Spirit should transcend all other human distinctions. In Him, believers are one body and external differences of language, race, culture, or class should not keep them apart.

## Abrahamic Epoch

1. *Abraham is the father of all believers.* This the apostle Paul makes unmistakably clear in the book of Galatians. "So those who have faith are blessed along with Abraham the man of faith" (Galatians 3:9). When God announced to Abraham that "all nations will be blessed through you," it was the "gospel in advance" (Galatians 3:8). So the gospel of Jesus Christ calls us into the inheritance of the promise to Abraham that God would be his God and the God of his descendants forever. "If you belong to Christ, then you are Abraham's seed, and heirs according to promise" (Galatians 3:29). In the person of Jesus Christ Abraham has indeed become a blessing to all nations. "He redeemed us in order that the blessing given to Abraham might come to the Gentiles through Jesus Christ" (Galatians 3:14). No wonder Jesus said, "Abraham rejoiced at the thought of seeing my day. He saw it and was glad" (John 8:56).

Abraham enjoyed a special friendship with God. He was called a friend of God. Through faith in Christ, believers from all nations may share in the special friendship Abraham knew. The Abrahamic covenant remains in force to be shared by believers everywhere. Nothing that followed its establishment, including the Mosaic law which came 400 plus years later, changed that.

The law, introduced 430 years later, does not set aside the covenant previously established by God and thus do away with the promise (Galatians 3:17).

Frequently Abraham's biological descendants mistakenly assumed that physical descent guaranteed them a special status before God. Thus John the Baptist warned, "Do not begin to say to yourselves, 'We have Abraham as our father.' For I tell you that out of these stones God can raise up children for Abraham" (John 3:9). Similarly Jesus said to those who had boasted of being Abraham's descendants, "If you were Abraham's children then you would do the things Abraham did" (John 8:39). True children of Abraham were those who shared Abraham's faith, regardless of the Jew or Gentile blood in their veins. And that faith centers in Jesus, says Paul, the true Seed of Abraham (Galatians 3:16).

As a matter of historical fact, the majority of Abraham's biological seed did not share his faith. Of his eight sons only one, Isaac, was a believer. Of scores of grandchildren only one, Jacob, was faithful. In Abraham's own household, his adopted servant Eliezer, born in Damascus, was the best model of one who shared his master's faith (Genesis 24:42-49). Yet Abraham's son Ishmael and grandson Esau who were biological descendants, were examples of unbelief and rejectors of Abraham's God. Throughout the two thousand years of Bible history until the coming of Christ, only a small minority of Abraham's physical descendants remained true to the Lord.

2. *The Privilege of being a Jew.* Yet it was an enormous privilege to be a biological descendant of Abraham. The apostle Paul asked the question, "What advantage, then, is there in being a Jew?" His answer? "First of all, they have been entrusted with the very words of God" (Romans 3:1 & 2). What an incredible privilege to be God's chosen agents to preserve and then communicate His word to the nations! And even more noble a honor to be the people who gave birth to the Living Word! "Salvation is from the Jews," said Jesus (John 4:22). Paul calls the gospel "the power of God for the salvation of everyone who believes: first for the Jew, then for the Gentile" (Romans 1:16).

The Jews were first not only as receivers of the Gospel, but also in bringing it to the nations. All of our Lord's disciples were Jews. The apostle Paul, who called himself "a Hebrew of Hebrews," was and remains the greatest missionary of the Gospel. The over-whelming majority of converts to the Christian faith during the first century of the Christian era were Jews. They were truly the first, and all nations which have been blessed with the Gospel of salvation in Jesus Christ should thank God for them.

In the book of Romans the apostle compares natural branches of a tree with unnatural branches grafted into the tree to illustrate the relation of Jew and Gentile (Romans 11:17-24). Both the natural branches and those grafted in receive their nourishment from the gracious promises given to the Old Testament believing community of faith and fulfilled in Christ. Today the believing remnant of Israel together with Gentile believers are the "new Israel," the new people of God, fulfilling the purpose for which the "old Israel" existed.

Gentile believers are described in Ephesians 2:12 as once "separated from Christ, excluded from citizenship in Israel and foreigners to the covenants of the promise, without hope and without God in the world." But Jesus Christ changed all that. The covenant family experienced a magnificent expansion. God inaugurated a new stage of the covenant without racial or national boundaries which includes all who believe in Jesus. Embracing all people to whom the Gospel has ever been proclaimed, Abraham's descendants are truly as numberless as the stars. "If you belong to Christ, then you are Abraham's seed and heirs according to promise" (Galatians 3:29).

3. *Circumcision as Covenant Sign.* When God promised to be Abraham's God and the God of his seed a sacrament was established to celebrate and serve as a reminder of this relationship. Infant sons of believers and adult male converts were circumcised to indicate that they were set apart for God's service. By means of Circumcision they carried the mark of God's ownership upon themselves. This covenant will never end (Genesis 17:7 "everlasting"). Believers in Jesus Christ share in this heritage as Abraham's spiritual children (Galatians 3:29). Jesus even spoke of one carried to heaven as in the company of Abraham (Luke 16:22). We would expect, therefore, that this continuing relationship would continue to include a sacrament to indicate and celebrate the blessing of inclusion within it. The New Testament revelation excels that of the Old by way of fulfillment and expansion in all regards. Strange indeed it would be if, in regard to a sacramental sign, those who are

the spiritual children of Abraham through faith in Christ Jesus should be denied what the children of Abraham before Christ had for two thousand years, namely, a sacrament of inclusion within the believing community.

Baptism is the sacrament both in meaning and purpose for which circumcision once served. The apostle Paul calls Baptism the circumcision of Christ. "In Him (Christ) you were also circumcised...having been buried with him in Baptism..." (Colossians 2:11 & 12). What Circumcision was, Baptism has become, to identify those set apart for God's service. Only the form of administration has changed. The form of administration *had* to change since blood shedding had lost its symbolic purpose once the perfect shedding of blood was done at Calvary. Now an unbloody sacrament serves as the sign and seal of the promise that once was sealed with a minor surgical procedure. Water now symbolizes the cleansing power of Jesus' blood. The everlasting covenant continues, and so does its confirming rite under a new form of administration.

True to the New Testament principle of expansion and greater inclusion within the orbit of promise and fulfillment, girls and women share in the sacrament of Baptism. Oneness in Christ does away with former distinctions which tended toward exclusions.

> For all of you who were baptized into Christ have clothed yourselves with Christ. There is neither Jew nor Greek, slave nor free, male nor female, for you are all one in Christ Jesus. If you belong to Christ, then you are Abraham's seed, and heirs according to the promise (Galatians 3:27-29).

The Old era was a time of indirect and subordinate participation by some segments of the believing community. It was a time for representatives to function on behalf of others. Priests represented the worshipping community in its ritual life. Sacrificed lambs on the altars represented the repentant worshippers acknowledging their need for atonement. Fathers represented the family unit in the governing councils of the covenant community. And boys and men represented girls and women in the Circumcision rite. But Christ has come, the perfect Representative anticipated by all the imperfect ones preceding. He is both Priest and Sacrifice, and no other representative mediators are needed. Now direct access and participation in worship, service, and sacrament is open to all.

The similarity between Circumcision and Baptism is even reflected in the similar tendencies toward on the one hand neglecting its practice, or on the other hand abusing its use. The people of the Old Covenant tended toward two common errors. They sometimes neglected to practice circumcision as God had required (Joshua 5:2-8). At other times they followed the practice out of form and habit when it meant nothing because the desire to consecrate themselves and their children to God's service was lacking. Without sincerity of commitment to the Lord the sacrament was meaningless. "Circumcise your hearts," says Moses to his stubbornly wayward people (Deuteronomy 10:16). Let the external sign indicate an internal reality! Similarly, Baptism is in danger of being neglected by some denominational traditions, while others baptize so indiscriminately that it is meaningless. If practiced sincerely, it is a precious reminder that God has laid His claim upon believers and their children. And they, in response, are called to faith and trust in Him who bought them.

*4. The Land of Canaan as an Eternal Possession.* How are we to understand, in New Testament light, God's promise to Abraham that he and his seed would possess Canaan? This is certainly a specific reference to a geographical area now known as Palestine or The Holy Land.

> The whole land of Canaan, where you are now an alien, I will give as an everlasting possession to you and your descendants after you; and I will be their God (Genesis 17:8).

If the promise was intended for the physical descendants of Abraham only, then Canaan can be claimed by both Arabs and Jews. They are all biologically related to Abraham through one of Abraham's eight sons; Hagar's son Ishmael (Genesis 16:15), Sarah's son Isaac (Genesis 21:2), and Keturah's six sons (Genesis 25:1).

The solution must be determined by the Bible's own identification of who are truly Abraham's seed. Earlier we observed Paul's definition of Abraham's descendants. "If you belong to Christ, then you are Abraham's seed, and heirs according to the promise" (Galatians 3:29). The promise included Canaan as an *everlasting* possession. How do believers in Jesus, both Jews and Gentiles, lay claim to possess that land? Not just in a temporary way either, but as an eternal claim?

All the promises to Abraham are fulfilled in Jesus Christ the perfect Seed of Abraham. In Christ all families of the earth are blessed. In Christ Abraham's seed are as numberless as the stars. So also the promise of the eternal possession by believers of Canaan must be seen in relationship to Jesus Christ. It is He who has made that land so special to believers. Jesus never traveled outside its territory except as an infant with His parents to Egypt. In Canaan He performed his healing and Kingdom-proclaiming ministry. There He died, was buried, arose from the grave, ascended into heaven, and sent His Holy Spirit at Pentecost. The redeemed from all nations will eternally look to that country as the place where their eternal salvation became reality. Canaan will always remain their special possession, their "holy land," the small territory on planet earth where God made good His promise to crush the head of the serpent. Centuries earlier the Psalmist had prophesied that people from many nations would be born again in Zion (Psalm 87). Eternally the saved will lay claim to that land as the place where their heavenly citizenship was earned. It will remain their eternal possession, the place where, in Christ, they were born again.

*Mosaic Epoch*

1. *Christ fulfilled Moses' testimony.* Jesus' own self-awareness of His relation to the revelation given through Moses was not one of contrast but of conformity and fulfillment.

> Do not think that I have come to abolish the Law and the Prophets; I have not come to abolish them but to fulfill them. I tell you the truth, until heaven and earth disappear, not the smallest letter, not the least stroke of a pen, will by any means disappear from the Law until everything is accomplished (Matthew 5:17 & 18).

In the parable of the rich man and Lazarus, Jesus implied that the witness of someone who returned from the dead could not be more convincing than Moses' writings (Luke 16:29-31). He further asserted to the unbelieving Jews that the Scriptures they so highly regarded could not be understood unless they were viewed in relation to Him.

> You diligently study the Scriptures because you think that by them you have eternal life. These are the Scriptures that testify about me, yet you refuse to come to me to have life

(John 5:39 & 40). If you believed Moses, you would believe me, for he wrote about me. But since you do not believe what he wrote, how are you going to believe what I say (John 5:45-47)?

The Gospel of Matthew especially demonstrates how Jesus fulfilled the revelation given through Moses. Some have suggested that Matthew's account of the life and ministry of Jesus was deliberately structured after the pattern of Israel's experience under Moses. The birth of Jesus corresponded to Israel's birth as a nation in the Exodus. Then followed the flight of Joseph and Mary with Jesus to Egypt and their eventual return to Palestine. This, says Matthew, fulfilled the prophecy, "Out of Egypt have I called my son" (Matthew 2:15). The baptism of Jesus in the Jordan paralleled the "baptism" of Israel in the Red Sea (Matthew 3). The temptation of Jesus (Matthew 4) recollected the temptation of Israel in the wilderness at Meribah (Exodus 17). Jesus' Sermon on the Mount (Matthew 5-7) became the new "Law" of Messiah's people corresponding with the Ten Commandments given through Moses at Mount Sinai (The Law on the Mount and the Sermon on the Mount).

These apparent parallels may be superficial and a bit forced. But one thing is certain, the burden of Matthew's gospel is to present Jesus as Israel's Messiah. He is the Divine Son for whom the corporate son, Israel, existed to bring forth. As the Divine Son, Christ lived in obedience to the Father like the corporate son should have, but didn't. Israel under Moses was supposed to be a Theocracy, a nation living under the rule of God. Jesus demonstrated both in His life and teachings what such a lifestyle would be like. His initial appeal was to "the lost sheep of Israel" (Matthew 10:6) to be the renewed theocratic people, citizens of the Kingdom of God. The nature of the Kingdom was taught by way of parables and the supremacy of the Kingdom was demonstrated through miracle power over disease, death, and demons (Matthew 10:8). In spite of such clear evidence of divine authority, the majority refused to respond with belief. They rejected Him and His message and crucified Him. Yet, a New Israel did emerge, and they, by the authority of the resurrected Lord, were commissioned to "go make disciples of all nations" (Matthew 28:19).

2. *Christ fulfilled the Law.* Three categories are distinguishable within the Mosaic Law, namely, Civil law, Ceremonial law, and

Moral law. Civil laws regulated the public life of the nation, establishing rules governing property rights, payment of debts, employer/employee relations, penalties for accidental or deliberate injury to others, and many other matters. Ceremonial laws governed the religious worship life of the community determining the appropriate religious sacrifices, feasts, and obligations that various periodic situations required. The Moral Law was presented especially in the Ten Commandments, and governed the ethical life of the people. It focused on the moral responsibility of the people in their relation to God and fellowmen.

Jesus fulfilled the Law in all three of its dimensions. The Civil law maintained the integrity of Israel as a people so that they could be preserved to give birth to the Messiah. With His coming the purpose for maintaining the continuity of Israel as a nation was realized and thus the civil injunctions were fulfilled. They had served their purpose and, therefore, ceased to be valid. Ceremonial laws anticipated the work of Messiah as the suffering Lamb of God who would atone for the sins of the world. After the Cross, Ceremonial laws ceased to be valid since their anticipatory function had been completed. The Moral law had its perfect expression in the Person of the Messiah. He fulfilled the requirements of the law whose essence always was to love God above all and fellowmen as oneself.

While the Civil and Ceremonial aspects of the Mosaic code had a provisional and temporary character and are no longer valid, the Moral law factor is still in force. This is so for two Biblical reasons: (1) the essence of the Moral law is love, and (2) the motive for obeying it is gratitude. Love and gratitude stand at the very center of the Biblical faith both before and after the completed work of Christ.

Moses impressed upon his own people the intimacy between love and obedience in relation to the Ten Commandments.

> Love the Lord your God with all your heart and with all your soul, and with all your strength. These commandments that I give you today are to be upon your hearts (Deuteronomy 6:5 & 6).

> Love your neighbor as yourself (Leviticus 19:18).

This same position is reflected in Jesus' summary of the Law (Matthew 22:37-40). The summaries of the Decalogue by Paul

(Romans 13:8-10) and James (James 2:8-12) clearly indicate their applicability to believers in the Gospel era. They both addressed New Testament Christians and summarized the Law to reinforce its continuing importance for them. The apostle John's reference to "commands" includes more but certainly embraces the Ten Commandments.

> This is how we know that we love the children of God: by loving God and carrying out his commands. This is love for God: to obey his commands (I John 5:2 & 3).

The introductory statement of the Ten Commandments not only identifies who God is but also indicates why His commandments ought to be obeyed. "I am the Lord your God, who brought you out of Egypt, out of the land of slavery" (Exodus 20:2). Gratitude for deliverance from bondage provides the motive for obedience. This is equally true for New Testament believers. Gratitude for deliverance from the bondage of sin and its consequences motivates loyalty to the will of Christ (I Corinthians 15:58; Hebrews 12:1-3).

3. *Passover anticipated Holy Communion.* The Sacrament of Passover was instituted at the time of Moses. For fifteen hundred years it commemorated the mighty act of divine deliverance from bondage. Jesus faithfully celebrated the Passover up to the night before He was crucified. That night He transformed it into the Supper of His remembrance, Holy Communion (Matthew 26:17-30).

The Passover meal included four major cups. Reflecting Exodus 6:6 & 7, these were called the cups of Sanctification ("I will bring you out"), Deliverance ("I will free you"), Redemption ("and will redeem you"), and Acceptance ("I will take you as my own people"). In Matthew's account of the Last Supper, only two cups, the second and the third, are mentioned, but these, according to early Jewish tradition, were the most important ones. The third was the most important of all. It represented the blood of the sacrificial lamb of the original Passover whose blood on the doorposts protected the residents from the vengeance of the angel of death (Exodus 12:13).

It was this third cup, the cup of redemption, also called the cup of blessing, which Jesus took and said, "This is my blood of the covenant which is poured out for many for the forgiveness of sins" (Matthew 26:28). The apostle Paul identifies this cup as "the cup of blessing" in I Corinthians 10:16. "The cup of blessing which we

bless, is it not a participation in the blood of Christ?" (RSV) Thus
the Lord's Supper essentially continues the celebration of divine
deliverance beginning with the Exodus under a revised form. The
mode of celebration *had* to change because the bloody sacrifice of a
lamb was no longer necessary. The perfect Lamb of God sacrificed
at Calvary fulfills all that the previous lambs symbolized.

We observed in chapter six that Passover was instituted as a lasting ordinance for all the ages to come (Exodus 12:17). Now we can
understand how Passover does indeed continue, under the modified
form of Holy Communion, for all generations. The message and
meaning are the same, redemption through the "blood of the
Lamb." It will endure into eternity itself, for our Lord said, at the
close of the Last Supper,

> I tell you, I will not drink of this fruit of the vine from now
> on until that day that I drink it anew with you in my Father's
> Kingdom (Matthew 26:29).

We see then that believers before Christ had an individual once-
in-a-lifetime sacrament (Circumcision) and a repeatable, communal sacrament (Passover). Likewise, the believing community
after the Cross continues to practice these rites under the forms of an
individual one-time Baptism, and a repeated, communal Lord's
Supper. Both of them have been given to identify participants with
God's people, reminding them that deliverance and salvation have
their source alone in the Lord. They are visual portrayals of the
Gospel. We see the water of Baptism and the wine of Communion
which symbolize the cleansing power of Christ's blood. We see the
broken bread which represents the broken body of our Lord Jesus
for our salvation. Together then, the preaching of the Word and the
administration of the sacraments engage all our senses. We hear the
Gospel preached with our ears, and we see, taste, feel, and even
smell the elements of the sacraments reminding us of the Good
News of salvation through Jesus Christ.

4. *Sabbath anticipated Sunday.* The point was made in chapter
six that, at the time of Moses, the Sabbath assumed a sacramental
character. That is, those who followed the practices regulating
Sabbath observance did so as a mark of identification with the community of faith. It fell on the seventh day of each week, appropri-
ately reflecting the revelational stance of the times. For the Old
Testament period was one of anticipation, looking ahead to the

fulfillment of promise, especially the promise of the Messiah. Thus the structure of the week reflected the direction of the movement of revelation, looking ahead six days to the reward of rest on the Sabbath.

But Jesus Christ changed all that. He came as fulfillment of all anticipations before Him. Now our revelational stance is one which looks back to the finished work of Jesus Christ, and the very structuring of the week reflects this. We begin each week resting in His grace and look back all week to the first day for our inspiration and assurance. Christ and His Cross is the point of transition so that the Sabbath requires first day celebration for the Christian. This explains why the first day of the week takes on such prominence in the New Testament. Notice especially the following references:

> The Resurrection occurred and Jesus appeared to His disciples on the first day of the week (John 20:19).

> Jesus reappeared one week after the Resurrection, the first day of the week (John 20:26).

> Pentecost, the day Jesus fulfilled His promise to send the Holy Spirit, took place on the first day of the week (Acts 2).

> Holy Communion was celebrated on the first day of the week (Acts 20:7).

> The Apostle instructs the Corinthian Church to receive offerings on the first day of the week, suggesting that fellowship meetings were held that day of the week (I Corinthians 16:1-2).

> The title "Lord's Day" was used to identify the first day of the week (Revelation 1:10). The term "Lord's Day" was already in use before the end of the first century A.D. It was an abbreviation of the phrase, "The day of the Lord's resurrection," which, as noted above, occured on the first day of the week.

5. *Christ, the perfect atonement for sin. Yom Kippur,* the "Day of Atonement", was the most solemn religious festival of the year under the Mosaic order (Leviticus 16). It was the only day annually in which the high priest could enter the Holy of Holies, the inner section of the Tabernacle. There God's presence was symbolized above the cover of the ark of the covenant, between the cherubim.

Elaborate preparation was required by the High Priest before he could enter the Holy of Holies. Two goats were carefully chosen, one to be slain, the other led away to die alone in the desert. With a bowl of blood drained from the slain goat, the High Priest entered the Holy of Holies. He sprinkled blood on the Mercy Seat, the lid of the ark, as atonement for the sins of the people. Between the symbolized presence of God above the Mercy Seat and the Law under the Mercy Seat was the atoning blood. It indicated that a sacrifice had been made vindicating the divine holiness and assuring mercy and forgiveness for those violating God's Law.

Above the head of the second goat the High Priest placed his hands symbolizing the placing of the confessed sins of the people upon the animal substitute. The goat was then led into the barren wilderness to die. It was the "scape goat" the innocent victim who carried the sins of the people away from the presence of God.

Chapter nine of the book of Hebrews focuses upon Good Friday as the ultimate *Yom Kippur,* to which all previous Day of Atonement festivals pointed. Christ was the true High Priest who brought the perfect Sacrifice to vindicate God's holiness. He carried his own blood into the heavenly Presence as payment in full for the sins of the world. He was also the Scape Goat, the Innocent One, who bore the sins of His people away from before the divine presence.

> For Christ did not enter a man-made sanctuary that was only a copy of the true one; he entered heaven itself, now to appear for us in God's presence. Nor did he enter heaven to offer himself again and again, the way the high priest enters the Most Holy Place every year with blood that is not his own (Hebrews 9:24 & 25).

> Christ was sacrificed once to take away the sins of many people; and he will appear a second time, not to bear sin, but to bring salvation to those who are waiting for him (Hebrews 9:28).

## Prophetic Epoch

Two themes run through the Messianic pronouncements of the Prophets, the Messiah as King, and Messiah as Suffering Servant of the Lord.

1. *The Kingly Messiah.* Matthew represents the Magi, visitors from eastern lands at the cradle of Jesus, asking, "Where is the one who has been born king of the Jews?" (Matthew 2:2). Then follows the description of the disturbed mind of King Herod at the news of One whom he saw as a potential rival. Matthew's contrast between two kings is too obvious to have been accidental. King Herod and King Jesus, an earthly and a heavenly monarch. What a contrast! Herod's kingdom was a typical earthly center of power. It was established by the sword, by spilling blood, other people's. Jesus would establish His Kingdom by shedding blood too - His own.

The comparison between the two kings appears to be terribly one-sided regardless of the side with which one identifies. By purely earthly standards, it appears to be one-sided in Herod's favor. His was the regal splendor of the Jerusalem palace with all the adornments of kingly power. But to the mind of faith the contrast is heavily weighted in Jesus' favor. In fact, he alone was a true Monarch. Even as an infant, though He had laid aside His glory, still He was King of kings and Lord of lords. All authority in heaven and earth was wielded by Him (Matthew 28:18). The real King, incongruous though it then appeared, was being fed at the breast of a teen-age virgin and destined for a cross.

No wonder the world has always had trouble understanding Jesus' Kingship. Love, humility, and self-sacrifice are not words associated with earthly rulers. Military and economic power, political intrigue, strategic diplomacy, these are the words typical of human government positions. But a Baby seems so irrelevant in the power equation of nations. The Holy Spirit opened the eyes of the Wise Men so that they would recognize the real King, and to accept that great paradox; the revelation of Divine power in utmost weakness. The Wise Men were not repelled by that apparent contradiction. Modern "wise men" are not all as wise as they.

But what was the shape of Christ's Kingdom? Negatively, it was not of the nature of earthly kingdoms. "Jesus said, My Kingdom is not of this world" (John 18:36). The prayer that Jesus taught His disciples identifies the essence of the Lord's Kingdom. "Your Kingdom come, your will be done on earth as it is in heaven" (Matthew 6:10). The Rule of God comes to expression wherever and whenever God's will is done. The reign of King Jesus is enlarged whenever someone is born again to join the ranks of those acknowledging His Lordship. Whenever a Christian institution is founded, the rule of Christ is given visible and concrete expression. Citizens of His Kingdom are freed from the allurement of relative and passing attachments which try to claim their allegiance. Their loyalties are above, resting in that which is permanent and abiding. They know that Christ is King, even though the final consummation of His Kingdom is still waiting. But slowly, sometimes almost imperceptibly, like a grain of mustard seed or yeast in a pan of dough, its promise is being realized. Until, one day, the vision of the last book in the Bible will have been realized.

> The Kingdom of the world has become the kingdom of our Lord and of his Christ, and he shall reign for ever and ever (Revelation 11:15).

2. *Messiah as Suffering Servant.* So intently focused were the people of Jesus' day upon the kingly portrayal of the messianic promise that they ignored or missed the prophesies concerning the Messiah as a Suffering Servant of Jahweh. They expected that Messiah, as David's greater Son, would restore the fortunes of national Israel. He would free them from all external political bondage and rule a utopia of political peace.

This false expectation of Messiah's rule was even shared by the disciples and close followers of our Lord. The mother of two disciples, James and John, implied as much by her request to Jesus on behalf of her sons. "Grant that one of these two sons of mine may sit at your right and the other at your left in your kingdom" (Matthew 20:21). The two sons obviously approved of their mother's request since the parallel passage in Mark 10:33-45 presents it as originating with James and John. They expected an earthly rule modeled after national organizational patterns and wanted to assure for themselves the inside track toward positions of prestige and power. This is clear from Jesus' response.

> Jesus called them together and said, "You know that the rulers of the Gentiles lord it over them, and their high officials exercise authority over them. Not so with you. Instead, whoever wants to become great among you must be your servant, and whoever wants to be first must be your slave - just as the Son of Man did not come to be served, but to serve, and to give his life a ransom for many" (Matthew 20:25-28).

Peter had a difficult time harmonizing his kingly expectations for Jesus with suffering and death. Jesus predicted his capture and mistreatment at the hands of the elders, chief priests, and teachers of the law, and their success in having him put to death (Matthew 16:21-23). "Unthinkable!" thought Peter. "Never, Lord!" he said. "This shall never happen to you" (Matthew 16:22). Peter was raised on stories of the Davidic monarchy and how it foreshadowed a greater Monarch to come. He could not square such an image of Messiah's rule with suffering and death. That element of the prophetic writings had passed him by or were simply ignored.

The prophet Isaiah presented the promise of a savior in both suffering and reigning terms. Messiah would be the One who, through suffering would attain unto ruling glory. Isaiah 53 represents the Messiah as "despised and rejected of men, a man of sorrows, and familiar with suffering." For those who, like sheep, have gone astray, he would be stricken, afflicted, pierced and wounded. He would be cut off from the land of the living and assigned a grave with the wicked. But *after* the suffering of his soul (verse 11) he would see the light of life and receive a portion among the great (verse 12).

Jesus draws together the two dimensions of His messianic work in His conversation with the two men from Emmaus.

> He said to them, "How foolish you are, and how slow of heart to believe all that the prophets have spoken! Did not the Christ have to suffer these things and then enter his glory?" And beginning with Moses and all the Prophets, he explained to them what was said in all the Scriptures concerning himself (Luke 24:25-27).

The prophet Zechariah spoke of the Messiah as the "Branch" who would be "a priest upon his throne" (Zechariah 6:13). That is, the Messiah would be both Priest and King, both sacrificer and ruler. Throughout the Prophetic Epoch the offices of priest and king were carefully separated. When king Uzziah arrogantly usurped the role of a priest he was punished with leprosy (II Chronicles 26:16-21). But Zechariah prophesied a time to come when a kingly descendant of David would be a priest ruling as king. Christ meets this prophetic expectation. He became the Priest who offered Himself as the perfect sacrifice to atone for the sins of all who believe in Him, and rules as King in the hearts of the redeemed. His Kingdom was founded on Calvary. The foundation of His rule is a cross. He is the King of Glory because He is the Lamb of God who takes away the sin of the world.

Jesus Christ is the one King who died for His subjects. He rules not to exploit but to bless, not to enslave, but to free. His faithful subjects are the privileged messengers of the Good News of the eternal Priest-King. They have been commissioned to carry the message of His grace and Kingdom to the whole world. And one day, it may be very soon, every knee will bow, and every tongue confess that He is Lord to the glory of God the Father.

## Discussion Stimulators, Chapter Eight

1. Reflect on the crucial importance of the use of words, both written and spoken, for effective communication. Why is the title "Word" so appropriate to identify Jesus Christ as Communicator of the person and will of God?

2. Adam, the first representative of humanity, produced a fallen human race. In the light of Romans 5:12-20 why is Jesus often called the Second Adam?

3. How did Jesus demonstrate the superiority of the Kingdom of God over the kingdom of evil?

4. What are some evidences that should be demonstrated among all Christians who share in common a unity in the Holy Spirit?

5. Relate the Covenant with Abraham, and its confirming sign, Circumcision, with New Testament believers and the sacrament of Baptism.

6. "All the promises to Abraham are fulfilled in Jesus Christ, the perfect Seed of Abraham." Explain.

7. Explain why, from a History of Redemption perspective, the Mosaic Civil and Ceremonial laws have been fulfilled and are, therefore, no longer valid. Why is the Moral law still in force?

8. How would you respond to someone who asked why Christians should celebrate Sabbath on the first day of the week?

9. Explain how Hebrews 9 presents the day of Christ's crucifixion as prefigured in the "Day of Atonement" of the Mosaic Ceremonial Law (Leviticus 16).

10. Why was it not a contradiction for the prophets to anticipate the Messiah both in kingly terms and in humiliating suffering terms?

### For Further Study:

Craig, S.G., *Jesus of Yesterday and Today,* (Philadelphia, Presbyterian and and Reformed, 1956).

De Graaf, S.G., *Promise and Deliverance,* (Philadelphia, P & R Press, 1979) III.

Vos, G., *Biblical Theology,* (Grand Rapids, Eerdmans, 1948) pp. 299-401.

# Textual Index